THE
REFORMED
EVANGELIST

THE
REFORMED
EVANGELIST

The Man, the Myth,
& the Message

AL BAKER & **RYAN DENTON**

SOLAS PRESS

Scripture quotations taken from the (NASB®) New American Standard Bible®, Copyright © 1960, 1971, 1977, 1995, 2020 by The Lockman Foundation. Used by permission. All rights reserved. www.lockman.org

Scripture taken from the New King James Version®. Copyright © 1982 by Thomas Nelson. Used by permission. All rights reserved.

Published by

SOLAS 5 PRESS

169 Alpine Drive
Shelbyville, KY
www.5solaspress.com

ISBN: 978-1-956258-01-1 (Hardback)
ISBN: 978-1-956258-02-8 (Paperback)
ISBN: 978-1-956258-03-5 (Ebook)

Printed in the United States of America

Contents

Foreword

When Jesus finished His great work of redemption—living a sin-free life in conformity to all of God's holy laws, laying down His life to satisfy divine justice against the sins of God's elect people, dying on the cross and being laid in a tomb, and then destroying death and bringing life and immortality to light through His gospel— He ascended upon high, led captivity captive, and gave gifts to men. In heavenly glory, our Lord reigns over the hearts of His redeemed people and He rules His church by His Word and Spirit. From that place ascended on high, Jesus continues to give special gifts to His church in the form of godly men. Ephesians 4:11-16 teaches this simple truth. Those specially made and specially gifted men are given by Jesus to His beloved church in the form of apostles, prophets, evangelists, pastors, and teachers.

The Christian church from the beginning has recognized the cessation of the offices of apostle and prophet, as well as the cessation of the miraculous authenticating sign and wonder gifts which accompanied the age in which those offices operated, particularly in the early chapters of the book of Acts. The entirety of the New Testament revelation which gives the historical account of the birth, life, miracles, cross-work, death, burial, resurrection, and ascension of Christ in the gospels, and then the theological explanation of who Jesus is and what He did in the epistles and letters has been completed. There is no need for the offices of apostle or prophet any longer. The canon of Scripture is closed and complete, and everything mankind needs to know about God, man, sin, grace, Jesus' person and work, salvation, judgment, heaven, hell, the law of God, the Christian life, etc. is contained in its sacred, God-breathed pages. The foundation-laying ministry of the apostles and prophets is complete. Paul said it so very clearly in 1 Corinthians 3:10-11, "According to the grace of God which was given to me, as a wise master builder I have laid the foundation, and another builds on it... For no other foundation can anyone lay than that which is laid, which is Jesus Christ."

The apostles and prophets laid that foundation by their extraordinary, miracle-working, and revelatory ministries. We, the ordinary ministers, build upon that already-laid foundation. That brings us to the subject of the book before you. Everyone agrees that we need pastors and teachers. But what about this office of evangelist? Many in the Reformed world see the office of evangelist as it is spoken of here—as an extraordinary office which has ceased along with apostle and prophet. Part 1 of this book makes the biblical case that the office is permanent as long as the Great Commission of our Lord remains unfinished. The argument for the cessation of the offices of apostle and prophet is easy to make. There is no need for those offices with the completion of the canon of Scripture. But how would one argue for the cessation of the office of evangelist when there is clearly so much work to be done in the evangelization and discipleship of the multitudes of lost mankind on earth? Part 1 is an excellent overview of the historical teachings of churches regarding evangelists as well as the view of many Reformed denominations and churches today. That brings me to one of the most compelling points of this book. I hope sincerely that everyone blessed to read it walks away with this point firmly in mind. That point is this: Jesus in His ascended glory gives the godly men that He does to His church for the purposes spelled out explicitly in Ephesians 4:12-14. Listen carefully to God's Word here. These are the purposes for which Jesus gives evangelists, pastors, and teachers to the church *today*:

> ...for the equipping of the saints for the work of ministry, for the edifying of the body of Christ, till we all come to the unity of the faith and of the knowledge of the Son of God, to a perfect man, to the measure of the stature of the fullness of Christ; that we should no longer be children, tossed to and fro and carried about with every wind of doctrine, by the trickery of men, in the cunning craftiness of deceitful plotting.

American Christianity has been plagued with a devastating double-whammy of Pelagianism and pragmatic revivalism. Pelagianism was the false teaching of the arch-heretic Pelagius who battled with Augustine, the great ancient doctor of grace, in the 5th century. Pelagianism taught that grace enables men to save themselves through the exercise of their own free will and works. This false teaching is perpetuated today through altar calls, the sinner's prayer, emotionalism, sentimentalism, carnal Christian teaching, and the like. Absent is clear, powerful preaching of the law of God accompanied by a forceful call to repentance and faith alone in Christ alone for the whole of one's salvation. Absent is the apostolic zeal for the biblical gospel which the apostle Paul clearly believed to be the doctrine of justification before God by belief alone in Christ alone completely apart from works done in or by the sinner. Pragmatic revivalism is using any and all techniques necessary to "get decisions," or what Charles G. Finney called "excitements of the senses" which are "fit to induce men to repentance." These techniques could include but are by no means limited to the likes of Aimee Semple McPherson flying on guy-wires through the air to her pulpit at Angelus Temple to preach in a Pilgrim costume from behind the steering wheel of the Mayflower, Billy Sunday (ex-baseball player turned evangelist) breaking chairs on stage and pretending to hit the devil out of the park with his baseball bat, Benny Hinn pretending to throw the Holy Spirit across a stadium knocking thousands of people off their feet to the floor, or Charles Finney researching the notoriously sinful townspeople prior to preaching to them so he could call them out by name for their sins and call them to what he called "the anxious bench" (precursor to today's altar call) in order to extract a "decision" from them no matter how many verses of "Just as I am" it took to get them to do it.

Amazingly enough, many if not most confessionally Reformed congregations borrow heavily from these methods. Why? Our theology mitigates against such things, doesn't it? Here is the point I hope everyone gets. *The American Christian Church has been like a child, tossed to and fro and carried about with every wind of doctrine, by the trickery of men, in the cunning craftiness of deceitful plotting* because we have discarded one of the permanent and necessary offices our ascended Lord on high continues to give to His church: Evangelist. Nearly every church has evangelists whether they acknowledge them, support them, encourage them, or ignore them as a nuisance. They're there because Jesus gives them to local churches. Every local church I have ever been in, whether they held evangelist to be a permanent office or not, had evangelists. There was always a group of folks who talked about and did evangelism all the time. Many in the churches looked at them as a bit odd. But it never occurred to most of us to consider that these men were in themselves gifts of Jesus to those local churches. What a sad irony it is indeed! While the Lord continues to give the church exactly what it needs in order to multiply disciples, evangelize communities biblically and faithfully, and plant churches, those often misunderstood men have been pushed aside so we can listen instead to charlatans like Finney, Sunday, Hybels, Warren, McPherson, and a host of others. The consequences have been catastrophic. Jesus gives evangelists to the church not merely to lead the way in actually doing evangelism. Jesus gives evangelists to His beloved church in order to prevent it from being tossed to and fro by every wind of doctrine regarding what evangelism is and how it is to be done. There has been in my lifetime over the past 25 years a resurgence of interest in and love for Reformed Theology. That has been a huge blessing and a much needed antidote to the doctrinal indifference and shallowness that plagues our nation's churches. While there has been an accompanying interest in evangelism, many start strong but quickly become discouraged. Part 2 addresses this issue. *What do evangelists do?*

The goal of evangelism is the glory of God, not the salvation of souls. Ironically, it is only when we see it this way that we will be faithful to the truth *no matter the results*. The same gospel that saved 3,000 people in Acts 2 gets Stephen killed in Acts 7. One point that is hammered throughout this book is that our Lord and His apostles as well as the early church did not use the "attraction" model of ministry. They did not get memberships at local gyms and frequent local coffee houses hoping to make friendships with people they might, after a couple of years, be able to speak to about spiritual things. They were deliberate and aggressive as well as clear and compassionate in their evangelistic work. Our goal is not conversions, although we pray and cry out to Christ for them. Our goal is the glory of God and faithfulness to that message, which we are promised throughout Scripture will often be met with great hostility and outright mockery. The temptation to soften the edges of the truth to make it more palatable to men is great in America where success is nearly always measured pragmatically in terms of numbers. Success in evangelism is unsaved people hearing the one true gospel clearly accompanied by a call to repentance and faith alone in Christ alone. We need evangelists to keep us on track with that truth so we are not distracted by the tumble-weeds of American revivalism which continue to blow in the wind all around us.

Parts 3 and 4 are wonderful practical advice for evangelists and churches punctuated by a very helpful look at the life, ministry, family, strengths, weaknesses, and trials of Cotton Mather. A heart for the lost, a heart for the glory of Christ's gospel, and a love for the local church will be the byproduct of a close walk with the Lord Jesus. In this terrible and often exhausting war with sin we call the Christian life, there are many pitfalls to avoid: sexual immorality, substance abuse, the love of money, pride, an unhealthy marriage, children, bitter-ness, bad health, laziness, mental health, and the devil himself. Those same old sins which broke David's bones are remedied by the same spiritual disciplines God's people have relied on since Adam fell and the gospel was announced to men in Eden. We must be a bible-saturated group if we are to be useful to God for the purpose of fulfilling the Great Commission. If we walk closely with Christ, all these things shall be added to us just as our Lord promised in Matthew 6:33. This section of the book is a wonderful encouragement to that end.

The book emphasizes the need for churches which have fallen asleep in the status quo to awaken and engage in serious soul-searching, self-examination, and repentance. After reading and soaking in this book for the past few weeks, I have come to a startling conclusion which is making it hard to sleep lately. One of the worst things that could ever happen to a church would be for it to bring in lots of money over budget every year, to have a faithful and large core group that attends every week, to have orthodox and biblical preaching, teaching, and doctrine, to faithfully follow the regulative principle of worship, to have vibrant services where people sing out with all their hearts to the Lord in worship, to have good marriages and men devoted to leading daily family worship in their homes, to have godly wives submissive to their husbands and encouraging them always to lead and be faithful, to have married men who love their wives as Jesus loves His church, to have children who are obedient and respectful to both their parents and church leaders, *but to have a congregation which as a whole has little or no heartache for the multitude of lost people all around us.* Everything listed in this last sentence is wonderful, don't get me wrong. I pray every day for all of those things. But evangelism has fallen on hard times in American Christianity. Keith Green wrote a song called *Asleep in the Light* about this very problem. The second verse goes: "*Oh bless me, Lord, bless me Lord, ya know it's all I ever hear. No one aches. No one hurts. No one even sheds one tear. But He cries, He weeps, He bleeds, and He cares for your needs. And you just lay back and keep soaking it in! Can't you see it's such sin!*" I have sensed a nagging sense of guilt in the hearts of all of Christ's disciples in every church I have been in since I was 18 years old. That guilt is because we rarely if ever baptize adult converts to the faith, but it is also because we rarely if ever actually *do* evangelism. The office of evangelist has not ceased because Jesus' church still needs it. In America today, the need for evangelists is greater than it has ever been. I pray that this book will receive a huge readership which will be as convicted and encouraged as I have been to stop talking about evangelism and start doing it, to look for the evangelists in my local church so we can get behind them and learn from them, and to pray more fervently for a great revival. To be equipped for this great work of evangelism, we need to embrace the evangelists that our dear ascended Lord on high sees fit to give as special gifts to local churches. There is much repentance that needs to happen in churches for how these men have not been supported, for how they have been mistreated, and for how they have been ignored. May our Lord in His grace raise up an army of evange-lists in our day and may they find comfort, encouragement, and a ready audience of teachable, humble Christian lay-people, pastors, deacons, and elders who will learn from them in their local churches so that none us of are like children, tossed to and fro by every wind of doctrine on how to do evangelism to the glory of Christ.

Pastor Patrick Hines
Bridwell Heights Presbyterian Church
Kingsport, TN

December 2021

Introduction

After laying down the doctrine of election in Romans 9-10, "Jacob I loved and Esau I hated," and that "God has mercy on whom He desires and He hardens whom He desires," Paul declares that "everyone who calls on the name of the Lord will be saved" and "how shall they call upon Him in whom they have not believed, and how shall they believe in Him whom they have never heard and how shall they hear without a preacher, and how shall they preach unless they are sent?" (Romans 10:14,15).

This book is about encouraging the work of evangelism in the world of Reformed theology. The doctrine of election should never mitigate evangelistic zeal. Rather, it should serve as a catalyst for fervent, intentional, and fruitful outreach among the lost. We desperately need Spirit-filled men who will go to the streets and pulpits of our cities and towns, preaching the good news of Jesus Christ—that He came to save sinners, to reconcile them to the Father by His death on the cross and His glorious resurrection. God made Jesus, who did not sin, to become sin on our behalf that we in turn might become the righteousness of God in Jesus Christ (2 Cor. 5:21).

But this enterprise of saving sinners has fallen on hard times in the United States. From 1990 to 2006, the U.S. population grew by 60 million people, yet church attendance increased by only half a million. No state in America is able to report a rate of church attendance which keeps up with its growing population. Of an estimated 400,000 churches in the United States, only 3.5 percent of them are seeing growth, and less than one percent of them are growing by conversion growth. To go further, nine out of ten churches in the U.S. are declining or growing at a slower rate than the population growth in their area. Very few adults are being baptized by profession of faith. This is especially true in our Reformed churches. The Evangelical church in the U.S. is in big trouble. Christine Wicker writes, "Evangelical Christianity in America is dying. The great Evangelical movements of today are not a vanguard. They are a remnant, unraveling at every edge. Look at it any way you like: conversions, baptisms, membership, retention, participation, giving, attendance, religious literacy, or effect on culture. All are down and dropping." The scene in England, Scotland, Wales, and Ireland is even worse.

John Dickerson writes of six downward trends in Evangelicalism which may in coming years render the Evangelical church in America all but extinct, or at the very least utterly irrelevant. Dickerson says that our numbers are greatly inflated. There are only around 26 million born-again believers in the United States. We are hated by our culture. We are divided amongst ourselves. We are facing economic ruin. We are bleeding out members. Thom Rainer suggests that as many as 20 percent of church attenders will not return to church after the Coronavirus pandemic is over.

Why is this happening in the Evangelical church? There are two reasons for our failure. The first is more general in nature and the second is more specific. First, almost every church in

America uses the "attraction" model of ministry in one form or another. This has been going on for well over fifty years. In the 1970's, the "church growth" model of ministry was popular. Pastors and church leaders studied the sociology and demographics of a community and sought to attract "homogeneous units" to their church, believing that people of the same culture and economic strata liked being with each other. Then the attraction model took on the "seeker friendly" approach. What does "Unchurched Harry" like? He enjoys skits and "how-to" messages. He enjoys advice on how to be more successful. We will adapt our churches to his tastes. Then, for a period of time, there was the emergent church model. The idea here was to be more authentic, to admit one's woundedness and vulnerability, and to make more use of formal liturgical worship which goes back to "the mystery" in the early church. Now we have the "mega-mega church," multi-site church campuses where the lead pastor through the use of hologram technology speaks to all the campuses at one time. These leaders have figured out how to give vast numbers of people what they want in church—therapeutic messages of self-improvement, little to no accountability, and professional entertainment to feed the desire to have a fun and uplifting experience. Consequently, the immorality which we see in our world is not much different from what we see in our churches. Divorce rates, abortions, and sexual promiscuity in the church are similar statistically as the non-churched.

The second reason for the demise of the Evangelical church is our failure to make use of evangelists in our churches. Paul the apostle tells the church at Ephesus that God gave some as apostles and some as prophets and some as evangelists and some as pastor-teachers for the equipping of the saints (Eph. 4:12-13). Our failure to use the God-ordained means of growing the church of our Lord Jesus Christ has wrought havoc in our day and will continue to do so unless we come to grips with the problem and make use of the remedy God has given us.

This book is meant to be an encouragement and stimulant for any Christian seeking to evangelize in a biblical way. It is also meant to be a corrective for certain incongruities that we see in the Western church today. Our prayer is that God will use it to clarify what the biblical office of evangelist is, and how it must be used in the church. Our prayer is that God will teach us, train us, and move us out to the world with the unsearchable riches of God's grace in the person and work of our Lord Jesus Christ, resulting in the transformation of millions of people in the United States and abroad. Not until evangelists are used in their proper capacity should we expect "the earth will be filled with the knowledge of the glory of the Lord, as the waters cover the sea" (Hab. 2:14).

PART 1

Theological
Foundations

The Reformed View of the Evangelist
(Historical)

We see in Scripture that God is the first and greatest evangelist. Directly after Adam's rebellion in the garden, God seeks him out with the question, "Where are you?" (Gen. 3:9). The same is true when the Son of God takes on flesh and dwells among us, coming to "seek and to save the lost" (Luke 19:10). It should not surprise us, then, that the last assignment given to the disciples before Christ's ascension is to "Go, therefore," and disciple the nations. Evangelize the lost. Call them out of hiding. Command them to repent and believe the gospel. Baptize them. These activities are all part of what it means to disciple the nations.

The Reformed church in general has never officially opposed evangelism. There were certainly pockets of Reformed believers who opposed George Whitefield, Jonathan Edwards, William Carey, and other "fanatics," but it was rarely argued that evangelism in itself is a bad thing. In fact, if anyone should be

3

confident about evangelism and its outcome, it should be the
Reformed believer. God is sovereign in salvation. God's sheep
will hear His voice and follow Him. God's means for bringing
in lost sheep is through fallible human beings preaching the
gospel. This is how God continues to build His church. It has
never failed. It will never fail.

Despite this unquestioned importance of evangelism among
the Reformed community in general, there has always existed
confusion about the actual office of evangelist. We often call
certain people evangelists or evangelistic while at the same time
denying such an office even exists. Reformed people recognize
George Whitefield as an "evangelist." J. I. Packer called Richard
Baxter "an evangelist."[1] When we use such descriptions, we
are acknowledging that these men had a particular gift for
evangelism, not that they held the official office of evangelist.
But herein lies the tension. Instinctively we know evangelists
exist and are important. On paper, as we will see, many in the
Reformed tradition deny that such an office is permanent. But
is this correct?

This chapter aims to shine a light at one of the greatest theological blind spots in Reformed history. The Reformed view of
the office of evangelist was erected on a faulty foundation and
needs to be reevaluated in light of Scripture and church practice. Our debt to John Calvin, John Owen, Matthew Henry,
and others in the Reformed tradition could not be overesti-
mated. They are rightly recognized as theological giants, and
we owe more to them than we will ever realize. But this is not
to say that they are inerrant, as we will see.

John Bunyan's *The Pilgrim Progress* (1678) features "The
Evangelist" as one of its most prominent characters. In the
opening scene of Bunyan's book, "Christian" has a Bible, but he
needs the Evangelist to help him interpret what he reads. More

---

1   J. I. Packer, "Introduction" to Richard Baxter's A Christian Directory (repr.; Ligonier, PA: Soli
     Deo Publications, 1990).

importantly, he needs the Evangelist's exhortation to persuade him to fly to Christ for salvation. Considering the influence such a book gives to "The Evangelist," it would be natural to assume that the Puritans in general regarded the office of evangelist as ongoing and highly important in their own day. This is far from true. The Puritans by and large believed that the office ceased with the Apostles. They claimed that such a view came from a close exegesis of Scripture, even though influenced by the Reformers and especially John Calvin.

Calvin, for instance, believed that the evangelists functioned as helpers of the apostles, though lower in rank.[2] He believed that Luke, Timothy, and Titus were examples of evangelists, as were the seventy disciples sent out in Luke 10:1: "After this the Lord appointed seventy-two others and sent them on ahead of him, two by two, into every town and place where he himself was about to go." The office was not permanent, although "the Lord has sometimes at a later period raised up evangelists...as has happened in our own day," which is a reference to Luther. But if Calvin thinks the evangelists functioned as helpers of the apostles, how is it that "the Lord has sometimes at a later period raised up evangelists," since the office of apostle has ceased? And how does Calvin conclude that Luther held the office of evangelist, especially considering that there was no formal or informal ordination of him to that office? And who decides who is and who is not an evangelist?

John Owen's treatment of the office of evangelist is lengthier than Calvin's, though similar in its conclusion.[3] The office was temporary. Its function was to serve Christ's personal ministry. Owen, too, believed that the seventy disciples were evangelists, especially since they were endowed with extraordinary

---

2   John Calvin, *Institutes of the Christian Religion*, ed. by John McNeill, tr. by Ford Lewis Battles (Philadelphia: Westminster Press, 1960), 4:1057.

3   The following three paragraphs come from John Owen, *The Work of the Spirit*. Ed, William H. Goold (1853; repr. Carlisle, PA: The Banner of Truth Trust, 1967), 445-453.

gifts. Owen describes them as "gospellers" or preachers of the gospel—distinct from ordinary teachers.

When Owen considers the roles of the seventy disciples, he notes three things that lend insight into who exactly he thought the evangelists were. First, they preached the gospel in all places. They did not reside long in any one area. Second, they worked miracles. Third, they helped to settle and complete churches, perhaps with someone like Timothy or Titus as examples. Owen also claims that the office is extraordinary because "not many will earnestly covet to be engaged in" its demands.

Owen concludes his remarks about the office by stating that it is unattainable today because there are no rules or directions for how to call an evangelist. Owen admits "this sort of man" is "obscurely delivered" in Scripture. If the Lord had meant for the office to continue, the Scriptures would have been clearer about what they were to do and how they were to be acknowledged or recognized. How does one go about recognizing an evangelist? What about ordaining an evangelist? And, having ordained the evangelist, what does he do? Owen also claims the evangelist is unnecessary today. Every church, planted and settled, is able to do the things that the evangelist had once been assigned to do. Now we have Scripture, pastors, and teachers to fill the role of the evangelist.

But is it proper to use an argument from silence to claim that a given office has ceased? We can state that the office of apostle and prophet has ceased not because of Scripture's silence on it, but because of its clear statement: "having been built on the foundation of the apostles and prophets, Christ Jesus Himself being the corner stone" (Eph. 2:20). The revelation of Christ has been given to us in Scripture. The foundation of the church is complete, hence the reason for the office of apostle and prophet to be temporary, not permanent. We no longer need revelatory gifts and offices. But Ephesians 2:20 makes no mention of the evangelist. Although Owen is correct to call the evangelist someone "obscurely delivered," it is far from correct to say that it is therefore an office that has ceased or is unnecessary. Plenty of important and permanent truths are "obscurely delivered" in Scripture. It is our job to figure out how to correctly interpret and apply such obscure truths to our current church context.

What about Owen's claim that the office has ceased because "not many will earnestly covet to be engaged in" its demands? Could we not say the same about the office of pastor and teacher? James himself warns against many wanting to become teachers (Js. 3:1). The work of pastor and teacher is demanding. It is often thankless. It rarely pays very well. Moreover, in our culture, the pastor and teacher are far from respected. It is not very desirable or something to be coveted. But is that a reason to claim that it is not perpetual?

Here we catch a glimpse of what is really going on as it pertains to the Reformed view of this office. The Reformers and Post-Reformers simply don't know what to do with this office. It sits in a kind of no-man's-land, somewhere between apostles and prophets on the one hand and pastors and teachers on the other. It is therefore easier to simply dismiss such an office, especially since the role of evangelism itself had not taken on official importance (methodologically) in the Reformed and Post-Reformed contexts.[4] Men like Owen and Calvin demonstrate profound exegetical acumen in most of their writings. Arguably, outside of Scripture, they have had a greater positive impact on the Reformed church than anyone in history. But here they are wrong.

Matthew Henry follows a similar line of argument as Calvin and Owen, albeit with important differences.[5] Henry claims that the evangelists were ordained persons, appealing to

---

4   "Official importance" is the key phrase here. This is not to imply that the Reformed and Post-Reformed churches did not evangelize. Far from it, they were busy turning Western Europe from the idolatry of Rome to the light of the true gospel. This is merely to point out that things like evangelists and evangelism methods were not in the forefront of topics at the time.

5   Matthew Henry, *Matthew Henry's Commentary* (1708-1710.; repr., Peabody, Mass: Hendrickson Publishers, 2003), 703.

2 Timothy 1:6 as a prooftext: "For this reason I remind you
to fan into flame the gift of God, which is in you through the
laying on of my hands." This disagrees with Owen, who argued
that one of the reasons the office has ceased was because there
was no clear idea on how to ordain them. Henry appeals to
Galatians 2:1 to show that the evangelists were companions
of the apostles: "Then after fourteen years I went up again to
Jerusalem with Barnabas, taking Titus along with me." Like
Owen, he claims that the evangelists were sent to settle and
establish churches. And, again like Owen, the evangelists were
not fixed to any particular place.

The Puritan Paul Baynes (1573-1617) has a slightly different
take, although in the main it is the same as Owen's.[6] Baynes
argues that the seventy were not evangelists. Christ's distribution of gifts to the different officers in the church happened
after Christ's ascension, not before, thus disqualifying the
seventy. He argues that either the evangelist was called immediately like Phillip, or he was called later on by an apostle, as
in the case of Timothy, Titus, Mark, Tychichus, and Sylvanus.
The evangelists were not apostles because they were called by
apostles. Also, the apostles were over all the churches, whereas
evangelists were only over some. Apostles founded churches,
whereas the evangelists helped to maintain them. The apostles
planted and the evangelists watered.

Here, too, we run into a difficulty with this interpretation.
It is often maintained the evangelists were merely helpers of the
apostles. Timothy is often put forth as an example. The idea is
that, because they were merely helpers of the apostles, once the
apostles ceased to be needed, so also were evangelists no longer
needed. Practically speaking, however, this simply can't be the
case. When Paul tells Timothy to "do the work of an evangelist" (2 Tim. 4:5), he is saying it under the assumption of Paul's

---

6   Paul Baynes, *Commentary upon the Whole Epistle of Saint Paul to the Ephesians* (1618; repr.,
     Stoke-on-Trent, England: Tentmaker Publications, 2001), 1617.

preeminent death. In other words, "after I am gone, Timothy, continue to do the work of an evangelist." Paul is not assuming that, once he is gone, the evangelist will no longer be needed. In fact, it could be argued that, especially now that the apostles and prophets are gone, evangelists are needed more than ever.

Samuel Rutherford provides another, somewhat unique reason for why the office of evangelist has ceased when writing to Richard Hooker on the subject of church polity: "If Richard Hooker have any ground from Eusebius or Scripture for evangelists now, or in Trajan's time, he must show that they have the gift of tongues: for how could evangelists be fellow-helpers to preach the Gospel to the Churches planted by the apostles if they were not an extraordinary office only?"[7]

There are several problems with this statement. First, to claim that contemporary evangelists have to have "the gift of tongues" is a requirement nowhere found in Scripture. Apostles spoke in tongues, but so did many lay Christians as well. Speaking in tongues did not qualify one as an apostle, prophet, evangelist, pastor, or teacher. In fact, in order to make such a claim, the same statement would have to be made for all Christians. For instance, would Rutherford claim that, because Christians in the days of the Apostles spoke in tongues after receiving the Holy Spirit, Christians today must therefore speak in tongues if they are to be rightly regarded as Christians? Second, although it is true that evangelists assisted the work of "the Churches planted by the apostles," the same must be said of the pastors and teachers as well. Rutherford would assumedly say, "True, but pastors and teachers are still needed in the church today. Where would the church be without them?" To which we would respond, exactly, which is true also of the office of evangelist. One of the church's tasks continues to be the evangelization of the lost. Not all of Christ's sheep have been brought

---

7   Samuel Rutherford, *A Survey of the Survey of that Summe of Church Discipline*, penned by Thomas Hooker (1658), 472.

into the fold yet. To say that pastors and teachers are needed in the church but evangelists are not is an irresponsible position to take.

What is obvious about the Reformed church's historical view of the evangelist is the confusion about exactly what this office is—or was. Each respective interpretation of the office differs from the others. But such confusion should not automatically disqualify such an office, especially considering the potential damage to the people of God if, as we will show, the office was never meant to be terminated. If the ascended Christ meant for the office of evangelist to be ongoing in His church, then to remove such an office would have devastating consequences on the body of Christ and the advancement of the gospel.

Another factor to consider is "The Church of England Controversy" which lasted into the nineteenth century. The Church of England claimed that Timothy and Titus were episcopal bishops, who they also saw as New Testament evangelists. They claimed the office of evangelist did not cease with the apostles but continued down to the present day in the person of bishop. This gave bishops an authorized status that would have made English Puritans uncomfortable—and frankly, us as well. Bishops in the Church of England were permitted to ordain ministers without consensus or agreement from any presbytery or local assembly. Decisions to ordain men to ministry positions were arbitrary and oftentimes despotic. English Puritans such as Thomas Cartwright and Scottish Presbyterians were quick to denounce such authority, since ordination should be a decision of many, not the decision of one man (we agree). But here too, the reason for excluding the office of evangelist was church politics, not exegesis of Scripture.

James Bannerman's view of the evangelist is influenced by this same controversy with the Episcopalian church.[8]

---

8   James Bannerman, *The Church of Christ* (1869; repr. Carlisle, PA: The Banner of Truth Trust, 2016), 756-764.

Bannerman believes Timothy held the office of evangelist, and that Titus "no doubt" belonged to the same office. Some of the duties which evangelists had in the Scriptures include carrying contributions from one church to another, conveying inspired letters from one Christian community to another, organizing infant churches, and remedying conflict and false doctrine in churches. His conclusions are based on the work which Timothy and Titus were expected to do.

In many ways Bannerman's treatment is the most thorough of those examined, but his angle of argument is irrelevant to the topic of whether the office is permanent or not. The reason for this is because of his opponents, who had determined that evangelists were to have the authority of bishops and permanently oversee selected churches. Thus, Bannerman shows that Timothy and Titus had ministries that were peripatetic, not settled—even though they would spend more time at one place than another as the need arose. Bannerman's other main argument is one already addressed—that because Timothy and Titus were attendants of the apostles, once the apostles passed out of use, so too would the office of evangelist. He describes Paul's attendants as

> a little band whose hearts the Lord had touched, and who were drawn to the apostle by the power of that strong personal attachment, and love, and admiration, which the character of Paul was so fitted to call forth from among the young, who followed him as the companions of his ministry and labours, and were at hand to bear his special commissions to whatever new quarter called for his interposition, or needed peculiar care—his representatives to the Churches in organizing their polity, in rectifying their disorders, in conveying to them his apostolic instructions, and in carrying out his apostolic decisions.

Like others, Bannerman includes as evangelists Tychicus, Epaphroditus, Mark, and Luke. He concludes "their office was extraordinary; their commission had its origin and its close in apostolic times; the position of the evangelists, like the positions of the apostles and the prophet, must be reckoned among those provisional arrangements of the primitive Church, which formed the transition to its permanent and settled condition." But is this really a good argument? Because they were close to Paul, they could have no official office once Paul ceased to exist? Does Paul's second letter to Timothy anywhere suggest this conclusion, or is it the opposite? Is not the main purpose of Paul's second letter to Timothy to bolster his faith and stoke his zeal for ministry even after Paul's demise? And consider again Bannerman's description of what the evangelists do: carry money from one church to another, convey inspired letters from one Christian group to another, organize infant churches, and remedy conflict and false doctrine in churches. Is there any reason to believe that any of these assignments would suddenly be unnecessary once the age of the apostles had ceased? Again, we conclude that Bannerman is grasping at straws when it comes to the office of evangelist.

It is well-established that the office of apostle and prophet has been replaced by Scripture. But what has replaced the office of evangelist? If it is the office of pastor and teacher, then why did the pastor and teacher not replace the office of evangelist when Paul wrote Ephesians 4? At what point did the office of evangelist become subsumed by the office of pastor and teacher, and where in Scripture would one find such an argument to support it? Calvin, Owen, Henry, and Bynes were pastors and teachers. They were not evangelists. As is common even today, pastors and teachers don't really know what to do with evangelists. It would be incoherent and absurd for the evangelist to say that the office of pastor and teacher has ceased because they don't understand such a role. It is equally incoherent for the pastor and teacher to say so about the office of evangelist. The Reformed and Post-Reformed remarks on the office of evangelist are comparatively brief and, if we are honest, arbitrary. But their view has been the tradition of the Reformed church ever since its conception.

John Bunyan's *Pilgrim Progress* provides the quintessential description of the biblical evangelist: "Christian saw the picture of a very grave person hung up against the wall; and this was the fashion of it. He had his eyes lifted up to heaven, the best of books was in his hand, the law of truth was written upon his lips, and the world was behind his back. He stood as if he pleaded with men and a crown of gold did hang over his head." Later on, Christian is told by the Interpreter that such a man "is one of a thousand; he can beget children, travail in birth with children and nurse them himself when they are born." Bunyan clearly regards the evangelist as essential. Considering the success of *Pilgrim's Progress* in both its day and ours, why did the office of evangelist fall into disuse, at least in more orthodox circles?

The reason for the Reformed church's decline in the early 1700's is multifaceted to be sure, but could it in part be because of a deficient view of the office of evangelist? Is it not ironic that it took evangelistic juggernauts like George Whitefield and the "New Side" Calvinists to jumpstart the sleepy church of the mid-1740s? And then, fifty years later, it took obvious evangelists like Samuel Davies and Asahel Nettleton to do the same? If we are honest with ourselves, could we say the Reformed church over the last 300 years has been defined by its robust evangelism, or is it the opposite? Are not the Arminians most identified with evangelism, while the Reformed church is more commonly identified with ivory tower aloofness? The next chapter will look more closely at the Reformed view of the evangelist today, asking whether we are using the office to its fullest and most biblical capacity.

The Reformed View
of the Evangelist
(Today)

Now that we have seen some of the ways the historical Reformed church has viewed the office of evangelist, we need to address some common questions and objections. To begin, we must admit that Reformed churches often given lip service to the ministry of the evangelist through statements in their books of polity, and yet the office has fallen into disuse.

For instance, the PCA *Book of Church Order* refers to evangelists in 5-3a, 8-6, and 21-11, respectively, describing their functions as a mission church pastor, a foreign missionary, and ministry intern. The OPC *Book of Church Order* says about the evangelist, "Since the gifts and functions of evangelists are necessary until the end of the age, this ministry is permanent and not confined to the apostolic period."[1] In the same chapter they describe it in the following way:

---

1   OPC *Book of Church Order*, 7-1.

The evangelist, in common with other ministers, is ordained to perform all the functions that belong to the sacred office of the minister. Yet distinctive to the function of the evangelist in his ministry of the gospel are the labors of (a) a missionary in a home or foreign mission field; (b) a stated supply or special preacher in churches to which he does not sustain a pastoral relation;...(d) an administrator of an agency for preaching the gospel...

But the caveat typically put forward by Reformed believers is that the evangelist operates as a function and gifting of the church, not as an officer. Sure there is such a thing as an evangelist, but this is not the same thing as pastor-teacher since the one is an officer in the church, the other is not. But what does it mean the evangelist is a function or gifting of the church and not an officer? What is the difference between a function and an office? Where can the distinction be found biblically?

Some Reformed churches give the church planter the "powers of evangelist" in order to receive new members into his church plant. Others will ordain or accept a man who is an elder and allow him to serve in a church as an evangelist. Others speak of the evangelist as having a function in the church, but not an office. When people attempt to dismiss the office, we are quick to say that the burden of proof is on the doubter. Show me in the Scriptures where this office was abrogated. There is no such evidence. Therefore, in a desire to be *ad fontes* (back to the sources), we look to the Scriptures for guidance on this and all other matters of importance, not our traditions. So, the first thing that needs to happen is for the office of evangelist to be acknowledged and used as such in our churches.[2]

---

2   See Dewey Roberts, "The Office of Evangelist" and "Are Evangelists Functionaries or Officers," vanguardpresbytery.com.

Back to the sources

Scripturally speaking, the most persuasive reason for the office of evangelist's perpetuity is that it is not mentioned as a foundational office in Ephesians 2. If God had meant the office of evangelist to be temporary or associated with apostles and prophets, it would have been included here. Paul also uses the phrase "apostles and prophets" in Ephesians 3:5, this time to indicate that the apostles and prophets were essential in revealing the mystery of the church. That mystery having now been revealed, the office of apostle and prophet are no longer necessary. But again, the office of evangelist is not included.

Ephesians 4:11 teaches there are four offices in the church, two of which have ceased, two of which have not. Two of the offices are foundational or revelatory, namely, apostles and prophets. Two of the offices are not foundational or revelatory, namely, evangelists and pastor-teachers. These offices are part of the building up of the church, which work continues from age to age. Also, as we have seen, Calvin himself notes that "where religion has broken down, He raises up evangelists apart from Church order, to restore the pure doctrine to its lost position." Calvin here teaches that evangelists, unlike apostles and prophets, can still be raised up and even fill an office in the church. Here Calvin shows himself to be more comfortable with evangelists and the office of evangelist than many modern-day Calvinists.

How is someone qualified to be an evangelist? For this we look to the same place we would for any other officer in the church: 1 Timothy 3 and Titus 1. Every evangelist should be an elder in his church, just as we would expect pastor-teachers to be elders. And when apostles and prophets were still around, we have reason to believe they also were elders. Peter says as much in his first epistle: "Therefore I exhort the elders among you, as your fellow elder and witness of the sufferings of Christ, and as a partaker also of the glory that is to be revealed." Thus, Peter was an apostle and an elder. Every apostle was an elder, but not every elder was an apostle. Peter's calling to the office of apostle was directly from Christ, as was the case for all the other apostles. As elders, though, the apostles had to fulfill the requirements for that office which are given in 1 Timothy 3:1-7 and Titus 1:5-9. They were both apostles *and* elders. The same is true of the evangelist. They are both evangelists and elders.

As we will see, evangelists are gifted differently than pastor-teachers, but they are still an officer in the church, and as an officer, they must pass the scrutiny of Paul's pastoral letters. Evangelists are not pastor-teachers, but rather are to work alongside the pastor-teacher to focus on the outward thrust of the church, just as pastor-teachers are gifted for the more internal aspects of the church. They are co-equals with different gifts and different focuses, but both are concerned for the household of God. Pastor-teachers are more inward focused. Evangelists are more outward focused. But both are necessary, and both must have a place in the leadership of the church.

The Scriptures teach that elder-qualified evangelists must lead the church to obey the command to "go into all the world and preach the gospel to all creation." Consider that in Matthew 9:35-38, the Lord said that the lost, who represent a plentiful harvest, were "sheep without a shepherd" and that workers were therefore needed to be sent into His harvest. The evangelist is, therefore, one who will shepherd. Secondly, Jesus' explicit command in Matthew 28:19-20 is that all that He commanded be taught to newly made disciples. The evangelist is, therefore, one who must be able to teach, which is the role of an elder. Finally, in 2 Timothy 4:11, the Apostle Paul admonished Timothy to do the work of an evangelist in fulfillment of his ministry. But Timothy was an elder. Thus, the office of evangelist must be filled by someone who is qualified according to the biblical standards used for any elder.[3]

---

3   Taken from the website of Reformation Frontline Missions, reformationfrontline.org.

The evangelist today

How does the Reformed church, whether Baptist, Continental, Independent, or Presbyterian, view the evangelist in today's world? We will address this issue by answering five questions: Who does the Reformed church think the evangelist is, what do they think he does, why do they think this way, what has resulted from their thinking, and what needs to happen next?

Most Reformed Christians today believe that the office of evangelist has gone the way of the offices of apostle and prophet, as we have seen. But we can go further and say that most in the Reformed church tend to view the evangelist as simplistic, even naive. I have heard these sentiments many times. They go like this: "George is a really good guy, loves the Lord and loves people. He has a zeal for God and a burden for souls, but he is just not very smart. His sermons are not very deep theologically, and he tends to skip over the technical exegesis of Greek and Hebrew words in the text. His preaching is just a little bit shallow, and most people seem not be fed by it. He paints everything in black and white. He does not seem to be aware of the complexities of modern day life. It is as though he thinks, 'God said it, I believe it, and that settles it.' Fine-tuned and nuanced arguments are not his strong suit."

People in the church also tend to think of him as unsophisticated, that the so-called evangelist seemingly has more in common with blue collar factory workers, or those who are less educated, and the fact that he often gets an "Amen" as they pass by, further proves in their mind that his style of ministry is only accepted among the "simple people." Of course, such a statement smacks of elitism, something God commands us to refrain from (James 2:1). When evangelists preach at churches or regional meetings of the church, few of those in the audience take their words very seriously.

The evangelists also tend to be too direct for the educated church officer or members. The sophisticated elitist is most often concerned with the evangelist's bold, sharp, no holds barred approach to evangelistic preaching and one-on-one evangelistic work in the neighborhood around the church, saying, "This is not the way we do things around here." From their perspective the evangelist lacks the wisdom of the world in knowing how best to reach the 21st century man. To the learned and erudite, the evangelist seems hopelessly simple and uncreative. "He needs more up-to-date methods," they say, but the evangelist is happy to go door-to-door in his community or preach the gospel on the streets, fully expecting to find people who are open to hearing the good news of eternal life and the forgiveness of sins through Christ's death and resurrection.

People in the church also like to say that the evangelist is pretty irrelevant. They claim that he looks totally out of sync with the secular people who hear him. When he stresses the nature of sin, naming some of the grosser ones like homosexuality and fornication, warning people that living without repentance will yield death away from the presence of the Lord and the glory of His power, some in the church roll their eyes. They are embarrassed by him. They are embarrassed for the church.

And finally, many in the church tend to view the evangelist as a rather threatening person. He seems over the top in his zeal. He brings up sin, judgment, and hell at the most inopportune times, like Thanksgiving Day dinner with all the extended family. Or, when he is asked to pray before a meal, he goes on and on about people's lost condition and apparently forgets that he is to pray only for the meal. And because of his direct manner of preaching, he often angers and alienates people. When he preaches at a funeral and mentions the awful reality of hell and the lake of fire, many think that he is over the top, beyond the pale, going to a place that is unpleasant in an already difficult time for the family of the person who has just died. People are very often angry with the evangelist. He speaks directly of sin, judgment, and the life to come and many simply do not want to hear his message. That's because the natural man does not receive the things of God, for they are foolishness to him (1 Cor. 2:14).

Do any of these characteristics ring true in your own life? If you are an evangelist, I bet you have experienced some of these comments or objections to your own ministry. And if you are not an evangelist, how many of these characteristics have caused you from time to time to wonder about the felicity or necessity of evangelists in the church?

What do Reformed people think the evangelist does?

Here, too, there are many misconceptions. They sometimes think that he stirs up unnecessary opposition to "more ordinary and conventional ways" of reaching people with the gospel. I remember preaching at Yale University several years ago when I saw a young man dressed up as a woman mocking us preachers, much to the delight of the student body watching the spectacle. A young freshman came up to me with tears in her eyes saying, "You people are ruining everything for us. We will never be able to reach these people now." I told her we were doing nothing other than what a famous alumnus of Yale (Jonathan Edwards) had done many years before, engaged in open air preaching.

They also think that the simple, bold style of many evangelists alienate people from the gospel. What they fail to realize, however, is that the gospel always divides. The unbeliever is at enmity with God, he is engaged in evil deeds, and hostile in his mind toward Him. That's because the unregenerate man has a cobra heart which spits venom at God and anyone else who stands for Him. Indeed, all who desire to live godly in Christ Jesus will be persecuted (2 Tim. 3:12). Perhaps the greatest display I have seen of outright hostility and hatred for the gospel has been while preaching at two Gay Pride Parades in St. Louis. Without ever mentioning the abominable sin of homosexuality, people were spewing hatred and vitriol at me, the other preachers, and ultimately at God.

They also tend to believe that evangelists act in angry and hateful ways, especially if mocked by the lost while evangelizing. Sometimes we engage the heckler, challenging his assertions or pushing back on his blasphemous words by warning him that he faces hellfire if he continues to live in that manner. Sometimes this seems harsh and cruel to the ordinary churchgoer. It seems that many in the church group all evangelists under the category "loose cannon." They tend to reject all open air preachers based on the one or two who give the craft a bad name. They tend to reject one-on-one workers for being too forthright when evangelizing strangers.

And one of the most common criticisms of the actions of evangelists is manipulating people into making a decision for Christ. To be sure, there are many who do this, but I have yet to find a Reformed evangelist who manipulates people into making a decision to follow Christ. A decision does not make anyone a Christian. Only the Holy Spirit can convict, regenerate, and lead someone to faith and repentance. While the evangelist should never be guilty of manipulation, he most certainly ought to engage in exhortation or motivation. The unbeliever must come to grips with his sin and he must run to Jesus for refuge.

Another unfair observation of Reformed evangelists is that they tend to bludgeon people. My friends, it is imperative that people come face-to-face with their sin, the heinous nature of it, and the eternal consequences to them if they die in their sins. An evangelist, of course, must make clear the unfathomable riches of God's grace in the finished work of the Lord Jesus Christ, but this grace must be contrasted with the sudden, terrifying expectation of judgment for anyone who fails to see his own sin and impending judgment by turning from it and running to Jesus for refuge. The evangelist, of course, must never be disrespectful or harsh, but he must be truthful.

I know many Reformed evangelists who are charged with being uncooperative with local pastors or campus ministers.

Does that happen from time to time? I am sure it does, but I also know that most pastors and college workers are not evangelists and therefore are often uneasy with any form of direct, intentional evangelism. In other words, there is probably very little, short of the evangelist abandoning his calling, which will satisfy most pastors and college workers. Evangelists should make an effort to work with pastors and college workers, but they must at the same time be faithful to their calling. Every now and then, someone will have a hankering to get involved in evangelistic ministry, but because it has not been approved by the elders or pastor, and because it does not fit the purview of their corporate model for ministry, the elders and pastors squash the idea. After being knocked back in line, the evangelist stumbles back into the pew to sit, listen, and write checks to keep the whole thing going.

And finally, Reformed evangelists are often accused of being a lone ranger, or someone without accountability. I know of several street preachers who long for their churches to support them, if not financially then at least prayerfully. Often, this does not happen. Some claim that because the man is not ordained, he should not be preaching. Most open air preachers we know would love to have accountability from their pastors and elders. However, there is also a danger in this. I know of at least one very fine, mature, and faithful open air preacher who apparently has been told by his elders not to engage in open air preaching any longer. He seems to be doing a lot of one-on-one work, but no preaching. I cannot understand how a pastor or elders can bind a man's conscience and forbid him to preach, unless of course he is under some sort to church censure.

Why do many in our Reformed churches think this way about evangelists?

First and foremost, again, most do not believe in the office of evangelist, nor the gift of evangelist. Most Reformed pastors love their theology and are good students of it. They love to preach doctrinally and exegetically-sound sermons, and their people love to listen to them. So, most Reformed churches are "heavy" on teaching but "light" on evangelism. Consequently, very few "unwashed" people make it to their churches, and as pointed out in the introduction, the way we are "doing church" is not working. We are losing ground big time. We must have a major paradigm shift, one which largely involves taking seriously the office of evangelist. We must find, recruit, train, and deploy evangelists into our communities, asking God to give us the conversion of millions of people.

Another reason most church leaders think negatively about evangelists is simply because of their own giftedness. Because pastors and elders are typically shepherds, they focus their attention on encouraging the believer, counseling him, visiting him in the hospital, and making sure he grows in his knowledge of the Bible. However, this is not the New Testament model. Every believer is a disciple, and every disciple is to multiply by actively engaging his community of friends and family with the claims of Jesus Christ. Our problem today is not only the attraction model of ministry but also our emphasis on addition rather than multiplication. Paul told Timothy that he was to teach the things he learned from him to other faithful men who would in turn teach others also (2 Tim. 2:2). A new believer is never told to stay in a theological incubator for seven or eight years before he is ready to minister. Paul told Titus to appoint elders in every city on the island of Crete and it is pretty clear that the church was very young, perhaps less than one year old by the time Paul wrote him. It is interesting to note that, in the verses immediately preceding the Great Commission in Matthew 28:18-20, Matthew tells us that some of the disciples bowed down and worshiped the risen Christ while others shrank back in doubt and fear, clearly double-minded about the work ahead. In other words, Paul did not wait to see who was at the time a true believer and who was not. He sent them out, trusting the regenerating work of the Spirit to make this plain in the days ahead. Jesus was on the move, and He expected His disciples to be on the move as well.

Church leaders also think negatively of evangelists because most believers, especially having been Christians for several years, have very few non-Christian friends or even acquaintances. So, living among unbelievers and being patient with their sinful lifestyles and worldviews in hopes of engaging them in the gospel is somewhat foreign to many believers. The problem with most of us who have been believers for a long period of time is that we have forgotten just how wicked and vile we were prior to our conversions. So, when leaders see evangelists spending most of their time with unbelievers, they think it is strange. These church leaders no doubt have seen people make professions of faith who have major problems financially or emotionally. The church has sought to help such people in the past and has been burned. So, some leaders think, "Been there, done that," and they are not interested in investing time and resources into such people.

Also, the Reformed church thinks poorly of evangelists because, like most of us, they cherish their security. They know believers in their church. They are comfortable with them. They look like them, dress like them, and have the same values as them. These new people have none of that. This shakes the status quo. Things can get kind of messy when new believers from the world come into the church. For example, let's say your evangelist led to faith in Christ a felon recently released from prison, or a homeless man. Let's say it was someone with hyper-charismatic tendencies. You can be sure that many in the church will be uncomfortable with such additions.

Probably the greatest reason, however, that many in the Reformed church are suspect of evangelists and do not give them their due is because, frankly, they are elitists. Now, this is a terrible sin. James told folks that they were never to regard their faith in the Lord Jesus Christ with an attitude of personal favoritism (James 2:1). The elitist thinks that he is a cut above everyone else. He is not at all impressed with the "simple minded" evangelist who believes we ought to put Jesus on the "scoreboard" of our conversations by telling people what we were like before we were converted, how this came about, and what difference it has made in our lives. At that point, the evangelist should ask, "Do you have a story like this?" If so, then he rejoices with the person. If not, he is ready to present Jesus to them. This kind of approach, however, makes most people in the church uncomfortable. It seems too straightforward to them.

The Reformed church thinks this way for at least two more reasons. First, they feel guilty. Pastors in particular know that they should be speaking the good news to whomever God places before them, but they rarely do so. Consequently, what we now see in the hip Reformed or Evangelical church is a change from "mission" to "missional." Mission is what the church once did—pray, intentionally evangelize by going door-to-door in a community, engage in street evangelism, and open air preaching. Knowing, however, that the church should do something but being unwilling to do what I just mentioned, they tend to move to the *missional* approach. That is, they hope to bring societal change, to bring "shalom" to the community, to make it a better place for everyone by serving the poor through soup kitchens, reading programs for children, and encouraging struggling artists to make their home in their church facility. None of these are necessarily wrong, but they are not making disciples, beginning with sharing the good news of salvation in Jesus Christ. So, the tendency is to move toward the point of least resistance, to be engaged in good work but not the best work.

And finally, many in the Reformed church think poorly of evangelists because they feel threatened by them. Consequently, they often lash out at them, distancing themselves from them, saying that this kind of ministry does not work in today's world, often citing how few people seem to come to faith through their efforts. These evangelists, however, are simply trying to be faithful to proclaim Jesus Christ and Him crucified anywhere, anytime, and any place.

What has resulted from these wrong ideas of the evangelist?

As we pointed out in the introduction, the Evangelical church, as well as the Reformed church, is shrinking. We are not keeping up even with our population growth. More and more people in our nation are living and dying without Jesus Christ and we know very well that Jesus is the only means by which anyone can be saved. This ought to severely grieve us. My friends, people in this country, not to mention the world, are dying and going into a Christless eternity where the fire is never quenched and the worm never dies.

Because there is a dearth of evangelistic outreach in our nation, we have continued to run headlong toward perdition. We are becoming more and more like Sodom and Gomorrah in Genesis, a people given over to unmentionable debauchery and perversion. Homosexuality, so-called same sex marriage, and gender dysphoria are all accepted and championed. The horse is already out of the barn. Not even conservative lawmakers will broach the subject of homosexuality. Then there is the evil of sex-trafficking, abortion, and the wholesale murder of many young people in our urban centers. The division in our country at this present time is palpable. Righteousness exalts a nation, but sin is a reproach to any people. The righteousness which once exalted our nation is all but gone, and that's because so few people are becoming Christians. The reason our nation was able to insist on self-government at the Constitutional Convention was because of the pervasive righteousness at that time due to the powerful preaching of George Whitefield and Jonathan Edwards a few years before. Evangelistic preaching which wrought hundreds of thousands of conversions was the catalyst for the founding of our nation.

To go further, the loss of evangelistic zeal is rapidly devolving into the dissolution of our republic. The early founders of our nation, while not all true believers (some were Deists), nonetheless knew that virtue or righteousness was vital to the success of self-government. People had to trust their leaders, and we can only trust righteous people. They further understood that true virtue can only come through sincere faith. And then sincere faith, which promotes virtue, yields true freedom, a freedom based on what people ought to do rather than the misconception that freedom is the ability to do whatever one wants to do. Simply put, a nation without morality cannot stand. Greed for power and money will taint the church, the family, the public sector of government, and the private sector of business.

And the neglect of the evangelist and what he brings "to the table," as it were, brings a compromised and worldly church. Why so? Whenever a church or pastor decides that they will seek to gain members by any unbiblical means is the moment they are on the road to watering down the message to gain a crowd, to build bigger buildings, to hire more staff, to have bigger budgets. A compromise on theology will always eventually produce a compromise on behavior, accepting licentiousness and wickedness into the church in order to be "compassionate." This is very obvious today in the issue facing many churches concerning so-called "Side B Homosexuality." The Evangelical church is allowing people who confess to be homosexuals to be not only members but ministers as long as they promise not to act on their perverse desires. Surely no Reformed pastor even twenty years ago would have acquiesced to this heresy, but here we are today in that very predicament.

The compromised church has also become a worldly church. We tend to ignore or gloss over the clear commands of Jesus to help the poor and needy. We tend to read into the prophet Amos a watered down version of his denunciations of those in Israel during Jeroboam's reign who were ripping off the poor with excessive rent charges or who were unjustly confiscating their property. Surely these commands and more should at the very least cause us discomfort and to ask the question, "Do I really need this big house? Couldn't I do with less so that I could give more money away for the sake of the gospel here and around the world?"

To make matters worse, our neglect of the office of evangelist and those gifted and called by God to evangelize has been exported to the rest of the world. Unfortunately, much of the church in Africa and India looks like us. They dress like us, build church buildings like us, sing American praise songs, and adopt our worldly prosperity gospel. And with all of this they also have partaken of our spiritual anemia. The American church is much like someone suffering from a lower than normal red blood cell count who is constantly exhausted and experiences headaches and shortness of breath. Such a person is alive, but persistent anemia could lead to death. In the same way, the American church is not yet dead, but surely she is exhausted with all our extraneous activity. There seems to be so little energy, so little power.

Because our population continues to grow rapidly, and since there are fewer and fewer new believers, especially in light of our explosive population growth, then in actual numbers those in America on the road to hell are increasing at warp speed. Surely this should concern every believer. Have we become so doctrinaire, smugly and coldly embracing the doctrine of election, that we have little or no concern for the lost all around us? Remember, almost 2 people die every second in this world. 108 people die every minute, 6480 every hour, 155,520 every day, and 56,764,800 every year.

And finally, our lack of zeal in supporting evangelists diminishes the glory of our great God as well as the person and work of our Lord Jesus Christ. The overarching theme of the Bible is, "I will be a God to you and you will be a people to Me." What a wonderful truth. God sought us when we were far from Him, and He revealed Himself in a saving fashion to us in the work of some evangelist. After all, our God is slow to anger and great in lovingkindness and compassion. He loves the world. He loves the sinner. Our failure to proclaim the excellencies of Christ and His finished work on Calvary's cross where He delivered us from the domain of darkness and brought us into His kingdom of light is the greatest travesty in today's western church. And the glorious work of preaching Christ crucified, making known His propitiating, sanctifying, justifying, and adopting death is neglected when we fail to make use of Biblical evangelists. Rioters in the streets, while severely mislead, nonetheless reveal something vital about our American psyche. People instinctively know change is necessary and they labor to produce it. Unfortunately, however, they are pursuing a pipe dream. The only hope for societal impact and transformation is the true conversion of millions of people and God has always used evangelists as His instrument in doing so.

Moving to a more Biblical model of evangelism

The Reformed churches must make a concerted effort to find, recruit, train, fund, and deploy evangelists. How can we find men gifted as evangelists? We need a paradigm shift in today's church. We must gain a vision to disciple disciple-makers. We must commit ourselves to a ministry of multiplication. We must challenge all believers to follow the Lord Jesus' command to all of His blood-bought people to get outside of our comfort zones and reach out to the lost around us. As we do, some will "rise" to the top. They will be the ones whom God gives conversions. An evangelist has an inborn desire to make Christ known to the lost. He has a burden for souls. He weeps over them in prayer. He cannot help but take every opportunity possible to engage someone in gospel conversations. But we must go further and think strategically of giving such men a vision of multiplication. As we find them and recruit them by giving them a vision for the future, then we can train them. How? We take them with us into the field. We model evangelistic activity to them. We give them attention by teaching them what they have just seen us do. We then watch them as we send them out to do what we have taught them. And then we let them go. We launch them out into the world, reminding them that they are to do the same with others. They are intentionally and volitionally to multiply their new fellow workers.

And then we must fund them. Churches should set aside a stipend or some modest amount to encourage the evangelists in their midst to apply their gift as much as possible. We do this for pastors and even missionaries. Why aren't we doing this for evangelists? While everyone is to do the work of an evangelist, not everyone in the church is an evangelist. Therefore, we need more men who can devote themselves full-time or nearly full-time in order to reach their community with the gospel of Jesus Christ. And finally, we must learn to deploy evangelists. An official laying on of hands can be very meaningful to those ordained to the office of evangelist. These men are set aside from ordinary affairs to give themselves totally with their teams to the work of making and multiplying disciples.

What do you think of the evangelist? Do you see the necessity of the office of evangelist? Has your view or attitude toward them been uncharitable? Will you support evangelists you know, both prayerfully and financially? Many of the evangelists I know would love to devote their entire day to preaching and doing one-on-one evangelistic work in their communities, but they must work another job to support their families. We need to take action. Learning more and reading more is okay as far as it goes, but what we need in today's western world is action. Will you consider the vital necessity of evangelists who train other evangelists who train other evangelists? Shall we not raise our sails, trusting the Holy Spirit to breathe on us the revival spirit we so desperately need?

What Every Christian Must Know about Evangelism

Every Christian must be clear on his own identity in light of the Great Commission (Mat. 28:18-20). Not every Christian will be called to the office of evangelist, but every Christian is called to evangelize. Just like not all Christians are called to the office of pastor and teacher, but every Christian is called to teach in some capacity—mothers teaching their children, husbands their wives, or Christian workers their co-workers.

The Ministry of Reconciliation

Perhaps the most obvious passage addressing the Christian's identity in the context of evangelism is in 2 Corinthians 5:16-21. In defending his apostleship against opponents who mocked his unimpressive appearance and weak oratory, Paul tells the Corinthians that if he seems to be crazy or out of his mind, it is for God. But if he seems to them to be of sound mind, it is for them. He then tells the Corinthians that the love of Christ is what controls, dominates, or drives him to risk everything to get the good news of Jesus to as many people as possible. He then says this:

> "Therefore from now on we recognize no one by the flesh; even though we have known Christ by the flesh, yet now we know Him in this way no longer. Therefore if anyone is in Christ, this person is a new creation; the old things passed away; behold, new things have come. Now all these things are from God, who reconciled us to Himself through Christ and gave us the ministry of reconciliation, namely, that God was in Christ reconciling the world to Himself, not counting their wrongdoings against them, and He has committed to us the word of reconciliation. Therefore, we are ambassadors for Christ, as though God were making an appeal through us; we beg you on behalf of Christ, be reconciled to God. He made Him who knew no sin to be sin in our behalf, so that we might become the righteousness of God in Him."

Let's take a brief look at this goldmine of information about the believer's identity found in this passage. The first thing we notice is Paul's totally new perspective. It is as though the blinders have come off his eyes. He tells us that he and Sylvanus no longer recognize people by the flesh. What does he mean by that? His flesh was a pretty big deal to him prior to meeting the glorified Christ on his way to Damascus to persecute more Christians. He tells us in Philippians 3:3-6 that we are the true circumcision, who worship in the Spirit of God and take pride in Christ Jesus, and put no confidence in the flesh, although I myself, he says, could boast as having confidence even in the flesh. If anyone else thinks he is confident in the flesh, I have more reason, he says: having been circumcised the eighth day, of the nation of Israel, of the tribe of Benjamin, a Hebrew of Hebrews; as to the Law, a Pharisee; as to zeal, a persecutor of the church; as to the righteousness which is in the Law, found blameless. Prior to his conversion, Paul had been a typical Jew, well-schooled, having privileges of wealth (not everyone had the chance of studying under Gamaliel) and Roman citizenship. His conversion, however, changed everything. From that point on he only saw two types of people in the world with only two potential eternal destinations. They were either in Christ our outside of Christ, and they were either on the road to heaven or the road to hell. Nothing else mattered to Paul at that point.

But we now direct your attention to three very obvious characteristics which are true of everyone born-again. The first one is found in verse 17. You are a new creation in Christ. "Therefore if anyone is in Christ, this person is a new creation; the old things passed away; behold, new things have come." Simply put, a Christian is a new creation. By whom? By God. He is the author of our salvation. Ezekiel refers to this as receiving a heart of flesh to replace the heart of stone (Ezek. 36:25-27). Jesus calls it being born-again (John 3:3ff). Peter refers to being born-again to a living hope through the resurrection of Jesus Christ from the dead (1 Pet. 1:3). And Paul reminds Titus that God saved us by the washing of regeneration and the renewing of the Holy Spirit (Titus 3:5). By being a new creation, this means everything has changed about you. You do not belong to yourself. You belong to Jesus. He bought you by His blood. He demands and expects your obedience, your unfailing faithfulness to Him. He has given you a new heart. Your old unregenerate heart loved sin, delighted in it, was enslaved by it. But now your new heart, the real you, loves God and hates sin. Consequently, you have new values, new motives, a new way of thinking, the capacity to live, speak, and act in ways totally contrary to how you once thought, spoke, and acted. The old way of thinking and living has passed away and the new way of doing so is now here. This is the reality of your new identity. This is all a supernatural work of grace. God did it. You are to accept it joyfully and live it out obediently.

Second, Paul also declares in verses 18 and 19 that Christians
are ministers of reconciliation: "Now all these things are from
God, who reconciled us to Himself through Christ and gave us
the ministry of reconciliation, namely, that God was in Christ
reconciling the world to Himself, not counting their wrongdo-
ings against them, and He has committed to us the word of reconciliation." Dear friends, let this glorious declaration from the
apostle sink into your heart and mind. You once were alienated,
hostile in mind, and engaged in evil deeds. Yet God reconciled
you to Himself through the fleshly body of Christ in His death.
Now he declares that you are holy, blameless, and beyond
reproach if you give evidence of following Him (Col. 1:21-23).

But what does it mean to be alienated from God? Consider
this illustration. Perhaps you know a young couple who were
married fifteen or twenty years ago, and they very much were
in love. They looked like the perfect couple, but as the years
rolled on, the pressures of the work world and rearing their
children began to take their toll on their time with each other.
They slowly drifted apart. The characteristics which previously
endeared them to one another began to be a point of irritation.
The husband forgot Paul's admonition to love his wife and
not be embittered against her (Col. 3:19), and the wife slowly
began to lose respect for her husband (Eph. 5:33). They have
become argumentative, even hateful in their speech with each
other. Finally, they both have had enough, and they mutually
agree to a divorce. They are hostile toward each other. They
are alienated from each other. They sit across a table with their
lawyers and decide how to carve up their assets and determine
custody of their children. They hate each other at that point.
But then something marvelous and amazing happens. They
become reconciled with each other. They repent of their sins
and wrongdoing, they ask for forgiveness and fire their attor-
neys, they tear up their divorce papers, and they begin to love
one another again. That's reconciliation on a human level.
But if you are indeed followers of our Lord Jesus Christ, you

have been reconciled on a much higher, deeper, and eternal level. You have been reconciled to your Creator, Sustainer, and Redeemer, and it happened because Jesus died for you and was raised again for you. We can also say that God, the Holy One, the consuming fire, has been reconciled to us. He was angry with us because of our sin but His wrath has been satisfied by Christ on the cross.

Therefore, because of this great work of reconciliation, Paul says that we are now ministers of reconciliation. Note that God has committed to us the word of reconciliation. We have no choice. This is not an option. We have been drafted into God's army. God has given us the word of reconciliation, and He clearly tells us what He means by the word of reconciliation. We are to declare to men everywhere that God has provided a way for hell-bound sinners, with whom He is angry, to be given peace with Him. This peace also is experienced in our ability to have peace with those whom we have wronged in the past or with those who have wronged us in the past. We can even have peace with ourselves in the removal of the guilt and condemnation we feel for our past deeds, speech, and thoughts.

But there is also one other identity characteristic we need to know about ourselves. This is found in verse 20: "Therefore, we are ambassadors for Christ, as though God were making an appeal through us; we beg you on behalf of Christ, be reconciled to God." We are ambassadors of our great king. What are the characteristics of an ambassador? First, an ambassador is appointed by his king or national leader. One does not himself choose to be an ambassador. Therefore, an ambassador serves at the bidding of his king and he represents the king in every way. He is never to act in a way which could undermine the king's authority or gravitas. He is to be above reproach. He is to give only his ruler's message. The ambassador is not free to give his own message, his own interpretation of the message, or his own spin on what the king has said or written. And the ambassador is to call the people to do what the king is requiring. It is clear that God has called every one of His people to represent His character and message before the world. We have no say in the matter. God has ordained it. Christians therefore are to follow in obedience all that the king is requiring, and we likewise are to encourage our audience to do the same.

Why is this vital and necessary? Paul gives us the answer in verse 21: "He made Him who knew no sin to be sin in our behalf, so that we might become the righteousness of God in Him." Paul declares to the Corinthians, as well as to us, that God has wrought a miracle of grace through our Lord Jesus Christ. The sinless, undefiled, perfect Son of God took upon Himself the sins of all His people and bore them on the cross. Why? For the purpose of making us righteous, without sin, before the Father. The sin and wrath which we deserve was placed on Jesus that we may be made right with God. All who are in Christ Jesus are new creations, reconcilers, and ambassadors. It is not enough to know these things, though that is vitally important. The end result of this amazing grace of God is to obediently serve our Lord and fellow man.

The Great Commission

The second thing we need to know is the Great Commission. Just prior to Jesus' ascension into heaven, He gave His disciples their very clear marching orders: "And Jesus came up and spoke to them, saying, 'All authority in heaven and on earth has been given to Me. Go, therefore, and make disciples of all the nations, baptizing them in the name of the Father and the Son and the Holy Spirit, teaching them to follow all that I commanded you; and behold, I am with you always, to the end of the age.'" Since there are always people who need the saving work of Christ applied to their souls, this Great Commission from Jesus is directed at every believer of every age. What does it mean? We find in verses 19 and 20 three participles and one aorist, imperative verb. This is very important, my friends, for the correct translation gives us vital insight into our marching orders from Jesus.

Verse 19 is generally translated, "Go." It sounds like a verb, yet it is not one. It is an aorist participle. Two present participles are also found in the text, namely baptizing and teaching. The only verb in the passage is disciple, which is an aorist imperative. Again, most translations get this wrong too. The Greek text does not say "make disciples" (this is how the NASB and the ESV render it). "Disciples" is not a noun. It is a verb in the Greek text. So, the text should read, "Having gone, disciple all the nations."

Think of it like this. A verb in the imperative mood gives you the command of the author, while the participles (words ending in *-ing* in English) tell you how to carry out the command. So, a command would be, "Clean up the kitchen." The participles tell us how to carry out the command—by clearing the table, by sweeping the floor, and by washing the dishes. Another command is, "Repair the car." How? By changing the oil, by changing the brakes, and by tuning the engine. We are commanded to "disciple the nations." How? By going, baptizing, and teaching. The aorist imperative verb form for "disciple" is emphatic. "Do it now! Don't delay! This is not a suggestion!"

I am also saying that baptizing and teaching are the two specific means by which we carry out the command to "disciple." Baptizing is a picture of regeneration, being baptized into the body of Christ (see Acts 2:38, Rom. 6:4, Col. 2:11, 12). By His atoning work on the cross, Christ reconciles us to Himself in His body that He might present us holy, blameless, and beyond reproach (Col. 1:22). It is also a means of identification with Christ, as Romans 6:1 makes clear. We have been buried with Christ through baptism into death so that we may walk in newness of life. Believers in Muslim cultures know very well that baptism can get them killed, since Muslims understand that the baptized person is leaving his former life behind and uniting with Jesus Christ.

"Teaching" is two-fold. It means giving information on how to live, and then exhorting us to obey those commands on holy living. Receiving the teaching from King Jesus is never enough. The end game is obedience, to actually do all that Jesus is commanding us to do. A disciple is someone who has been born-again, who has the heart of Jesus in regenerating grace, who has been baptized into the church. And he consequently is one who is learning the ways of God found in His word and who is seeking to obey those commands every day of his life.

The marching order for every Christian, then, is this: "Having gone into the world (since it is assumed that you are already going), disciple all the nations." How? We are to evangelize everywhere, and we are to instruct believers to obey God's word. Anything beyond this is secondary or tertiary.

The Demoniac

And thirdly, we must know that God is calling us to go to "our people" and tell them of the great things God has done for us and how He has shown us mercy. We see this vividly played out in Jesus' dealing with the Gerasene demoniac (Mark 5:1-20). During His early Galilean ministry, when Jesus was working out of Capernaum, located on the northwest shore of the Sea of Galilee, He got into a boat with His disciples and sailed to the southwest shore to the region of the Gerasenes. These were Gentile, pagan, uncircumcised people who had no Bible, who were strangers to the covenants of promise and excluded from the Commonwealth of Israel. They had no hope, and they were without God in this world. We know they were Gentiles because the text later tells us they were pig herders. Jews would never raise pigs. We also know from history that they were under the oppressive boot of the Roman Empire and, no doubt, the pig herders were making a nice living selling pork to the Roman legions in the area.

As Jesus disembarked from the boat a man with an unclean spirit met him. What kind of man was he? He was a loner, living amongst the tombs, in a cemetery, which the Jews always considered an unclean place. No doubt the family of this man had tried to help him for many years, but they had grown tired of trying, much like a family finally gives up on a sibling or son who is hooked on drugs or alcohol and has cost the family untold dollars and emotional duress. This demon possessed man had preternatural strength. Broken shackles and chains hung from his arms and feet. No one was able to subdue him. He was exceedingly self-destructive. He gashed himself with stones. His body was covered with wounds. We know that he was naked and that he went amongst the tombs and in the surrounding mountains screaming at the top of his lungs. This demon possessed man was no normal man. He was under the influence of demons. He was over the top, beyond the pale. He is the worst case of demonic possession in the Bible. No one else comes close to him.

When he saw Jesus, the man immediately ran up to Jesus and bowed down before Him. Try to picture the scene. This wild, strong, naked, demon possessed man runs at Jesus, screaming at the highest decibel imaginable. At the very least, we would give ground to this man. But Jesus did not. He wasn't intimidated by him. The demoniac referred to our Lord as "Jesus, Son of the Most High God." The man knew who Jesus was. This was a threat, like someone saying to you, "I know who you are and I know where you live." Three times the man implores, begs, and tries to make Jesus swear that He will not torment him or destroy him. The man tells Jesus his name is *Legion*, for there were many demons in him. No doubt the man had seen many legions of Roman soldiers. A Roman Legion consisted of six hundred foot soldiers and one hundred and twenty horsemen. Roman soldiers were always exceedingly well organized. So are the demons. They come after people using all their means to tempt and destroy them.

As the exchange continued between the demon possessed man and Jesus, the man implored Jesus not to send him out of the country but rather into the nearby pigs, which Jesus does. The two-thousand pigs immediately rushed down the steep bank next and drowned in the sea. The herdsmen ran into the city and surrounding areas telling everyone what had happened. When they returned, they saw the man sitting down, clothed, and in his right mind. They were terrified. Who is this Jesus? The people asked Jesus to leave the area since the pig herders were very upset at losing their source of revenue. They were likely unsettled by a man with such power.

But the demoniac was wonderfully, drastically, and gloriously saved. He was never the same. He witnessed the demise of the pigs and with them the demons. The man knew that he would never again have to deal with them. He was a new creation in Christ. He was free from sin, Satan, death, hell, and the lake of fire. Jesus manifested His mighty power over the devil.

The man was so thrilled with Jesus and what He had done for him that he asked if he could follow Him and be one of His disciples. But Jesus said, "Go home to your people and report to them what great things the Lord has done for you, and how He had mercy on you." The man obeyed and went throughout his region telling everyone what great things Jesus had done for him.

Dear readers, have you forgotten what great things God has done for you? You have been justified, redeemed, cleansed, chosen, blessed, sealed, adopted, sanctified, delivered, predestined, foreknown, filled, empowered, seated, and one day you will be glorified. God is calling us to go to "our people" and tell them the great things God has done for us. Who are your people? You can begin with your own family and extended family. Then make a list of your neighbors, friends (even your childhood friends whom you have not seen for many years), and work associates. Then begin praying for them. Ask the Lord to put on your heart a burden for a few of them and then, in obedience to Jesus, go to them. At the very least you can tell them of what you were like before you were saved, how God saved you, and how your life has changed since that time. You can also talk of a special trial you faced. And then you can ask them, "Do you have a similar story?" If the answer is "No," then ask them if you can share the good news of Jesus with them.

Fourthly, we need to know the truth about people who are still dead in their sins. Let these haunting words sink into your heart and change the way you live: "When the Lord Jesus will be revealed from heaven with His mighty angels in flaming fire, dealing out retribution to those who do not know God, and to those who do not obey the gospel of our Lord Jesus. These people will pay the penalty of eternal destruction, away from the presence of the Lord and from the glory of His power" (2 Thes. 1:8-9). All have sinned and fallen short of God's glory. All are storing up for themselves the just and righteous judgment of God on all their thoughts, words, and deeds. God will by no means leave the guilty unpunished. Our God is a consuming fire. He is a God of divine retribution. Well over fifty-five million people die each year worldwide. Many of them die without Christ and suffer the eternal, conscious torment of hell. Christ is their only remedy.

PART 2

The Call to Arms

The Need for
Evangelists Today

Thus far we have sought to show the Reformed view of the office of the evangelist in the church, both historically and today. We have also demonstrated what every Christian must know about evangelism. Now we take up the issue of the need for evangelists. On the one hand this chapter may seem unnecessary. We know of some in the Reformed world who believe that the ordinary means of grace, namely holiness of life, traditional Reformed worship and sacraments, and the faithful exposition of the word of God from the pulpit is sufficient to build the church and convert the world. We have also seen that many in the Reformed world believe the office of evangelist no longer exists. And if it no longer exists, then it is not hard to see how these same people would also deem the office unnecessary. After all, if God has deemed something no longer in use, then obviously it is no longer necessary.

Our intent throughout this book is to be *ad fontes*, to go back to the source of the Bible—God's holy, inerrant, inspired, and infallible revelation to man. So what does God tell us about today's need for evangelists? We will address this by asking four basic questions and giving each an answer with four parts. First, what should every Christian know about evangelism? Secondly, what should every Christian do about evangelism? Thirdly, are these things currently happening? And fourthly, what needs to happen when it comes to evangelism?

What should every Christian do about evangelism?

First, we need to observe what Jesus told His apostles to do. In Matthew 10, Jesus sent the twelve out to preach the kingdom of God and to heal people and cast out demons. In Luke 10, He sent out the seventy to do the same thing. He told them to make disciples of all nations by going, baptizing, and teaching them to observe all that He had commanded them to do. He told them to preach the good news of the kingdom to all the nations, beginning in Jerusalem. They were to wait, however, until they had received power from on high. That power came ten days later at Pentecost. He told them to be His witnesses when they received that power. There is no question on what they were to do. The apostles were called to preach the kingdom of God. They were to take up their cross daily and follow Him. They were to deny themselves. They were to confess Him before men. They needed to know that if they were ashamed of Jesus then He would be ashamed of them.

We can go further to say that the extended family of believers, the one hundred and twenty praying in the Upper Room, were also to be His witnesses. At Pentecost they were bearing witness of Christ's glorious resurrection to the assembled Jewish contingent in Jerusalem. In Acts 8:4, after their dispersal from Jerusalem, the disciples went about "gospelizing," or talking about the good news of Jesus. All the believers must have continued this great work of proclaiming Jesus because Paul reminds the Romans that their faith is known throughout the world (Rom. 1:8). He told the Thessalonians that there was no need for him to say anything more in Thessalonica because they were upholding the gospel witness (1 Thes. 1:8). He told the Colossian believers the same thing (Col. 1:6). And in his first epistle, Peter is addressing the exiled believers from Pontus, Galatia, Bithynia, and Cappadocia and says that all of them are to proclaim the excellencies of Him who called them out of darkness into the marvelous light. They were once not His people but now they are His people. They once had not been shown mercy but now they had been shown mercy (1 Pet. 2:9-10).

So what should every Christian do? He must evangelize daily. He must tell those around him the great and mighty things God has done for him. He must proclaim how He has had mercy on their souls and will do the same for anyone who calls upon the name of the Lord to save them.

Are we obeying Jesus?

D. James Kennedy once said that about five percent of Christians actually share their faith. Only around one percent of all the churches in America are actually growing by conversion alone. So the answer is clear. We are not obeying Jesus' command to disciple the world by going, baptizing, and teaching them to obey what Jesus has taught. This raises a further question—why are we not evangelizing? Why are the vast majority of American believers unwilling to speak publicly and openly about Jesus?

First, many in our churches are likely not true followers of Jesus Christ. That's a pretty bold statement, but the previous statement supports our claim. Failing to evangelize is a serious red flag. Jesus and the apostles, as well as the disciples who followed called people everywhere to repent and return to the Lord. The Lord commands us to do the same. An unwillingness to obey a king is treason. Jesus is our king. Therefore, our disobedience proves that we are refusing to acknowledge Him as such. Jesus said that if we love Him then we will keep His commandments (John 14:15).

Second, there is a problem of "hyper-grace" in our churches today. Yes, our God is gracious and patient with His people. But this gives us no license to flaunt our disobedience by disregarding His specific demands about evangelism. A true believer has the life of God in his soul, and he will do all he can to submit to the One who has shown him mercy. A man who constantly tells his wife of his love for her but who continues in infidelity is a liar and a cheat. Likewise, those who proclaim their love for Jesus but who casually and constantly live in unrepentant sin (like not evangelizing) betray their confession.

Since unregenerate people have not the heart of Jesus, they also lack a Biblical vision, passion, and mission. Earlier we referred to Paul whose pre-conversion vision was his religious and fleshly pedigree. He learned after meeting Jesus on the road to Damascus that the old had passed away, and that the new had come. His new vision was not the educated versus non-educated, nor Jew versus Gentile, nor rich versus poor. Rather, it was that people are either in Christ or they are not; they are on the road to heaven, or they are not. Many in the church today seem to have a faulty view of people. They see them as rich or poor, white or black, woke or non-woke, oppressed or the oppressor. Jesus and His disciples saw them as saved or unsaved, lost or found, on the way to heaven or hell.

These folks also seem to lack passion to see people converted. Again, Paul is a good example of the contrast. He previously was about his pedigree and religious status, but after his conversion he was ready and willing to count them all rubbish, or manure, in order to gain Christ and to be found in Him, not having a righteousness of his own but rather the righteousness of Christ Jesus which had been imputed to him by faith. Consequently, he was able to say without hesitation, "The love of Christ controls or dominates me." And because of this love of Christ, he had a Biblical sense of mission. Paul had been a violent persecutor, oppressor, and blasphemer, but God had shown him mercy. This former persecutor became the great apostle and church planter who in less than ten years produced church planting footholds in four Roman provinces. He is the same man who apparently after his first imprisonment in Rome produced a church planting movement in Illyricum, Nicopolis, Crete, and Spain (see Rom. 15:19, 24, Titus 1:5, 3:12). All of us have a myriad of earthly responsibilities and cannot be expected to give ourselves "24-7" to evangelism and planting churches. But this should not mitigate our zeal to see the good news of Jesus Christ published to all the world in whatever capacity the Lord places us. All true followers of the Lord Jesus will have a passion for the Great Commission.

A third reason we are not obeying Jesus' command to disciple the nations is because the western church is more geared toward programs, money, buildings, staffing, and what many are calling the "attraction" model for ministry. The moment any pastor or elder goes down that road is the moment he has opened himself up to compromise. He has decided he will live by the motto, "the end justifies the means." Despite having a true concern for the lost and a desire to reach them, the church leadership decides that fidelity to the Bible can either be ignored or loosened. They convince themselves that today is a new day, that what worked fifty years ago will not work today, that new measures are justified. So, enormous sums of money are spent on buildings, multi-staffing, exotic ministries to children and youth, and doing all they can to entertain the lost. And often these schemes work in the sense that they bring many people into the church, so it seems "successful." But at what cost? The congregation becomes the spectator watching the professionals carry out a musical, drama, or teaching ministry. This is not the Great Commission, nor is it church. The flock comes out once a week to give money, sit amongst the crowd, listen to an uplifting, often psychotherapeutic message, and slip away until the next weekend. The church member becomes quite content at sitting, soaking, and soaring. This is similar to sheets and towels that get washed, but never get put into the dryer. Two days later you go to your laundry room to wash your t-shirts and socks and realize your neglect. Now you have to deal with the soured sheets and towels all over again. The Apostle Peter made clear that all of us are to proclaim the excellencies of Him who called us out of darkness into His marvelous light. We are to be actively engaged in the ministry of evangelism.

What needs to happen?

In light of the fact that every Christian is called to evangelize, but few are doing it, what needs to happen? The answer is straightforward. We must have evangelists. To understand this, consider that we need to recapture a kingdom-oriented dimension to our salvation. Jesus did not simply save us from our sins and from hell. Yes, He did do that and it is glorious and we must never forget it, but He did not begin with that. Matthew tells us that Jesus began by proclaiming, "Repent, for the kingdom of heaven is at hand" (Mat. 4:17). Mark records Jesus saying, "The time is fulfilled, and the kingdom of God is at hand: repent and believe in the gospel" (Mark 1:15). After preaching from Isaiah 61 in the synagogue, and after healing many people, Luke tells us that Jesus said, "I must preach the kingdom of God to the other cities also, for I was sent for this purpose" (Luke 4:43). Jesus announced that He was the long-ago prophesied Messiah, the King of Israel, the Son of David, and He was sent to bring in His Father's kingdom. Among other things, this means that the rule and reign of mercy, grace, justice, and effectual power had come to the world in the incarnation of Jesus.

When a king conquered a new nation, he always sent his ambassadors to the newly conquered people to announce the terms of their subjugation. The people knew to obey lest they perish in their rebellion. Jesus comes to people every day through His evangelists who are to announce that a "new sheriff is in town." The people have a choice. They can obey and live or they can rebel and die. Paul made the same idea clear in his Areopagus address when he said to the Athenian power brokers, "God is now declaring to all men everywhere that they must repent for He has fixed a day in which He will judge the world in righteousness through the One He has appointed, having furnished proof by raising Him from the dead" (Acts 17:30, 31). And what are the first words Jesus gave His disciples after He had spoken with them? "Follow Me." Not *believe in Me*. Not *come to Me*. Not *trust Me*, but *follow Me*. And from that command to follow He promised that He would make them fishers of men (Mat. 4:19).

And if we are to get to the place where we see that we must have evangelists, then we must also realize, as we have already noted, that everyone of us are to be evangelists. To go further, every one of us are to be disciple makers. There is no Biblical evidence for a two-tier disciple system for believers. Today we hear of people becoming Christians, of deciding to follow Jesus but who continue to live in carnality, who never seem to make any progress in Biblical holiness. Then we seem to hear of a second tier of believers who for some reason really get turned on to Jesus and really want to follow and serve Him, which includes evangelism. But what does Jesus say? "If anyone wishes to follow Me then he must deny himself, take up his cross daily, and follow Me." He says that, unless a grain of wheat falls into the ground and dies, it will not bear fruit. Christians bear fruit, which means that (among other things) they evangelize.

The command to disciple the nations applies to everyone of us. So, if we are to reach the growing number of millions and millions of people in our country who are lost and on their way to hell, then we must have a paradigm shift. We must begin to take note of our great responsibility, all of us, to become disciple makers. We will never win the day doing the same things we have been doing for hundreds of years. Adding a church here and there, adding a few new converts every couple of years to our churches, will never get the job done. Every believer must see himself as a disciple and a disciple maker.

But how can we expect this to happen? If Christians begin to think more Biblically, an amazing thing will happen. The ordinary church member will become unleashed from his ecclesiastical shackles and move outside the walls of the local church building and engage in ministry. He won't think of Christianity as something you do on Sundays, and even then, it is only the professionals who actually do the teaching, discipling, and evangelizing. Christians must be unleashed with the gospel upon their communities, places of work, and in their homes. There are thousands and maybe millions of believers in the West whom Christ has gifted by the Holy Spirit to be evangelists, but who have been languishing in the pew because the church doesn't know what to do with them. Although all are called to evangelize, these evangelists will lead the charge. Others will be teachers or shepherds. Others will be bent toward mercy ministry to the poor and needy. All are relevant and all are needed. We are seeing a growing number of Reformed evangelists who preach on the streets, on college campuses, at sporting events, court houses, and abortion clinics. Others do so through door knocking or one-on-one work.

God has always raised up evangelists. These men are the spearpoint to any effective ministry. They go out, much like Paul and Barnabas did as they were sent out by the elders at Antioch and become missionary bands. They preach in the open air. They engage in door-to-door evangelism. They engage people through Bible studies. They use all manner of means to see people converted. They are like the obstetrician who brings the baby into the world. After he has finished his task, the obstetrician moves onto the next woman in labor and delivers her baby as well. The elders and pastors are like the pediatrician. They are responsible for the new baby Christian growing to maturity. And every pediatrician has assistants in the office to make his or her work run more smoothly. The deacons and others with mercy ministry gifts and gifts of logistics help the elders and pastors carry out their God given tasks.

When Al married his wife many years ago, God gave them three living sons. Each of them married in due time and had their own children. So now, from the two of them there are a total of twenty. And when their children are grown and have their own children, our numbers will no doubt double or triple. You get the picture. We must be about the business of Christ's kingdom which is multiplying believers. Evangelists are the starting point for such ministry. Our present failure in the western church is because we have failed to engage in the Great Commission the way God has ordained us to. If we follow His plan, thousands of evangelists can be unleashed into our communities, encouraging others to follow their lead. From this, we can expect to see a profound spiritual awakening.

What Does
the Evangelist Do?

Now that we have seen the deficiency in both historical and contemporary Reformed thought as it pertains to the office of evangelist, we need to figure out what exactly an evangelist does. If we were to talk about the duties of pastoral ministry, we could include preaching to the flock, shepherding, counseling, discipling, administering the sacraments, and protecting the church. But the role of the evangelist is not so clear, primarily because not as much thought has been given to it. If evangelists still exist as official officers, what are they supposed to do? How are they different from other officers in the church? Charles Hodge's comments on the office of evangelist are useful for our purposes here:

> "They were properly missionaries sent to preach the Gospel where it had not been previously known. This is the commonly held view, in favor of which may be urged—1. The signification of the word, which in itself means nothing more than preacher of the Gospel.

2. Philip was an evangelist, but was in no sense a vicar of the apostles; and when Timothy was exhorted to do the work of an evangelist, the exhortation was simply to be a faithful preacher of the Gospel. Acts 21, 8; Eph. 4, 11; and 2 Tim. 4, 5, are the only passages in which the word occurs, and in not one of them does the connection or any other consideration demand any other meaning than the one commonly assigned to it. 3. Euangelisthai and didaskein are both used to express the act of making known the Gospel where it had not been heard, and an instructor of those already Christians."[1]

We would disagree that evangelists and missionaries are synonymous roles, since missionaries are typically involved exclusively in church planting and pastoring, despite the obvious fact that evangelism will be needed as well. Evangelists are not necessarily involved in church planting or pastoring, even though it is possible that they do both. But Hodge indirectly brings up an important question about the office of evangelist—what does an evangelist do? They are "gospellers" to be sure, or people who share the gospel with the lost. But every Christian is called to do this. Evangelists are to "make known the gospel where it had not been heard." But people who are not evangelists in the official sense of the term can and should do this as well. Think of people at work or school who speak of Christ to people who have never heard about Him. This was the difficulty with which Calvin, Owen, Matthew Henry, and the other theologians wrestled. If the office is ongoing, surely it would be clear about what the evangelist would do. So, where should we turn to find out some answers?

---

1   Charles Hodge, *Commentary on the Epistle to the Ephesians* (Tappan, New Jersey: Fleming H. Revell, n.d.), 225.

Equipping the saints

Paul states in Ephesians 4:12 that the role of the evangelist is to "equip the saints for the work of ministry," in this case, the ministry of evangelism. Evangelists, by gifting, have a passion to teach about evangelism. But they don't teach the lost about evangelism. They teach the saints. In a similar way that pastors and teachers discuss hermeneutical principles or certain passages of Scripture with relish, so evangelists can talk about evangelistic methods and ways to reach the lost for hours. This is what we should expect when the ascended Christ gives this calling to certain men. Far from being the only ones who go out to evangelize, they would lead and teach the saints to evangelize themselves. Although the evangelist by his very calling would be desirous to evangelize, it is specifically his task to teach the saints to do the work that sets this call apart from others.

Paul states in Ephesians 4:14 that another purpose of being equipped by evangelists is "so that we may no longer be children, tossed to and fro by the waves and carried about by every wind of doctrine, by human cunning, by craftiness in deceitful schemes." When such a statement is applied to evangelism, it becomes obvious how a deficient view of the office of the evangelist has played a crucial role in why the Evangelical church has been so poisoned by pragmatism and unbiblical views of evangelism and missions in the last 200 years. The church has been "tossed to and fro by the waves and carried about by every wind of doctrine" when it comes to evangelism. Pastors and teachers are crucial for protecting the flock, but they can only do so much. They can't possibly keep up with the changing methodologies of evangelism when they have other topics to keep up with that are just as important. So, what happens when an entire office is shut out of the church, assuming it is an office that Christ never intended to cease existing? Without biblical, elder-qualified evangelists teaching the saints how to do evangelism, and more specifically, how not to do evangelism, the church has opened itself up to devastating consequences. We

see this today in the form of easy-believism, revivalism, emotionalism, gimmicks, and pragmatism. These are typically the
most common approaches to evangelism, even in the Reformed
church. But have we not brought this upon ourselves by excluding the voice of the evangelist inside our churches? We assume
the evangelist is primarily for ministry outside the church walls,
whereas Ephesians 4:11-16 shows that the opposite is true.

Hence, the primary role of the evangelist is to equip the
saints to do the work of evangelism. This can be done through
trainings, Bible studies, sermons, or intentional outreaches
designed for the purpose of equipping. The evangelist is called
to help protect the saints from evangelism methods that could
be described as "crafty" or "deceitful." They are called to ground
the saints in robust, biblical approaches to evangelism. This in
itself indicates how important evangelism is to the ascended
Christ. He has set aside an entire office to make sure the saints
are instructed, protected, and encouraged in this area. In a
similar way, it indicates how detrimental it is for this office to
be overlooked, or worse, made defunct by the church.

It should be noted that, biblically speaking, evangelists are
not rovers or itinerants. It is true that Philip initially seems to
be zipping back and forth to different locations in Acts. But
later on, we see that he is settled and has a house and family.
Evangelists are called to equip the saints in the local churches.
In order to do so, they won't typically have an itinerant role.
This is a far cry from what we see Billy Graham or Billy Sunday
doing. There may be times when the evangelist is needed more
at a particular church or location than another and, hence, will
relocate to help the respective area. There may be times when
a particular evangelist is called to oversee church planting and
evangelism in a large swath of territory either domestically
or abroad. But this is much different than assuming that the
evangelist would be in any way disconnected to any particular
church or churches.

Ideally and biblically, the evangelist should be an officer of the church. He should be included as part of church leadership. He should be an elder. This is rarely the case, however. Sometimes it is because the aspiring evangelist does not meet the requirements as given in 1 Timothy 3 and Titus 1. In this case, the fault is with the evangelist, not the church. He should be diligent about growing in maturity for the purposes of seeing more fruit in his ministry, but most importantly, because it is the duty of every Christian. Most times, the reason the evangelist is not included in the leadership of the church is because the church does not have a high view of the office of evangelist. In this case, the fault would be with the church. This is not to say that the evangelist should leave his church in pursuit of another. Sometimes that may be necessary, but even more helpful would be for the evangelist to work patiently with his leaders to show the biblical value of including an evangelist in church leadership. This can be difficult. It may be more frustrating than even evangelizing the lost. It may not produce favorable outcomes. But it is biblical. It is Christ-like. And oftentimes, the leadership will come around.

Gospelizing the lost

Another, more obvious job of the evangelist is gospel proclamation to the lost. A good example of this description is found in Vanguard Presbytery's *Book of Church Order*. "Evangelists sound forth the message of redemption in the destitute parts of the Church and superintend the work of systematic evangelization."[2] They are gospel preachers to both the lost and "the destitute parts of the church." Also, evangelists "superintend" or lead systematic evangelization to the lost, which would be in agreement with the idea of equipping the saints "for the work of ministry." This idea is also picked up later on in the Vanguard *Book of Church Order*: "The evangelist is he whom

---

2   12-1

the Church doth appoint to labor in its aggressive work."[3] They are spearpoints for intentional evangelism. The evangelist as an ordained officer in the church can "administer the sacraments in foreign countries, frontier settlements, or the destitute parts of the church."[4] The Orthodox Presbyterian Church states something similar in chapter 7 of its *Book of Church Order*:

> "The evangelist, in common with other ministers, is ordained to perform all the functions that belong to the sacred office of the minister. Yet distinctive to the function of the evangelist in his ministry of the gospel are the labors of (a) a missionary in a home or foreign mission field; (b) a stated supply or special preacher in churches to which he does not sustain a pastoral relation; ... (d) an administrator of an agency for preaching the gospel..."

The evangelist must be one who does evangelism. As mentioned above, every Christian is called to evangelize, but the evangelist should be doing it more than anyone else. Whether open air preaching, door knocking, one-on-one conversations, or handing out tracts in malls or public parks—evangelists must evangelize. How can the evangelist equip the saints to evangelize if he isn't doing it himself? This in itself will be an instrumental boost to equip the saints for the ministry of evangelism. When the saints see the passion of the evangelist, they will be inspired to do it themselves. Evangelism should be taught from the pulpit and in the classrooms. It should be studied in the Scriptures and other books. The hard part, however, is moving from the church or study into actual evangelism. The evangelist will be instrumental in encouraging the saints to evangelize when they see him doing the work. This does not mean that every Christian will be excited about evangelism or even an

---

3   12-3

4   12-3

evangelist in their midst. The evangelist should not have false expectations. Like any minister, the evangelist will face opposition both outside and within the church. But the best way to overcome such opposition is by evangelizing in season and out of season, which is also the best way to encourage others to evangelize.

Evangelistic literature

Another way a person could serve as an evangelist is through writing and distributing evangelistic literature. Gospel tracts have to be written by someone, so why not an evangelist? It goes without saying that not all evangelists will be gifted writers, so this is not for everyone. Someone who knows how to use evangelistic literature is not the same thing as knowing how to write evangelistically. Evangelistic literature could also include books on certain topics that specifically address the lost. Another way to serve as an evangelist could be through formal or informal apologetics. Paul the Apostle often debated unbelievers, and when done biblically, it can be very effective. Arranging debates online on biblical topics could be a way to expose the inconsistency of an unbeliever's worldview, while at the same time showing the consistency of Christianity. It could prove to be an excellent opportunity for a clear explanation of the gospel. Not every evangelist will be drawn to engage in formal apologetics, but it nonetheless should be considered evangelism.

One of the basic and foundational doctrines of Reformed theology is the fact that God has chosen a people for Himself before the foundation of the world. Paul the Apostle makes this clear in many places, including Ephesians 1:3-14, Romans 8:28-31, and Romans 9:14-18. Jesus speaks of the same thing in John 6 when He says that all the Father has given Him will come to Him and those who come to Him, God will in no way cast them out of His presence. I often pray and encourage others to pray for a mighty work of revival in our nation, one which produces millions of conversions. I am convinced that unless

God does this great work then we are doomed as a nation. The question, however, is how shall this work come to fruition? If you wish to go to the ocean and sail, then two things are necessary. First, you must have wind. Without wind, you are going nowhere. You are totally dependent on the wind for having an environment where sailing is possible. The wind is like the Holy Spirit in the work of the gospel. Without the sovereign work of the Spirit, nothing will happen. Second, you can have a nice wind kicking up when you are in your sailboat, but then what? You have a responsibility. You must lift up your sails. Until you do so, you still are going nowhere. The lifting up of the sails is the specific, tangible, and necessary work of evangelism. So, God has many people in our cities whom He has chosen and for whom the Lord Jesus died. Our job is to pray for laborers for the harvest and we must also, as evangelists, train others to go out into the harvest.

Making disciples

This brings me to another vital point. We must learn to multiply leaders. Paul makes this clear in 2 Timothy 2:2 where he tells his prodigy, "The things you have learned from me in the presence of many witnesses, these entrust to faithful men who will be able to teach others also." Most of us have mentored or even discipled individuals from time to time, and this work has been helpful to those with whom we have spent our time. This is good, but is it Biblical? Is it enough? Is that what we see Paul telling Timothy to do? It is not enough to make a disciple or church leader and be content with that person growing to a greater measure of spiritual maturity. No, we must go further. We are to multiply disciples. As evangelists, we must intentionally work to disciple the disciple makers. What would happen if evangelists made a concerted effort to find faithful men to disciple, who will then disciple others, who will also disciple others to three and four generations of disciples? How powerful would that be? What if every evangelist was discipling at least one or two other men, especially those more evangelistically minded? Therefore, we need a major paradigm shift in today's Reformed churches and even among Reformed evangelists. Knowledge of theology is good, but it does not go far enough. Evangelizing the lost is good, but it oftentimes stops short of the goal. We must have the multiplication of disciples and the multiplication of evangelists in today's world if we are to see our nation transformed.

Furthermore, we must not be guilty of putting form before function. The church is often guilty of this. Yes, Paul laid down the teaching on qualifications for elders (1 Tim. 3:1-13, Titus 1:5-9), but this form came long after the function of disciple-making and church planting had begun. Paul had finished his third missionary journey around AD 58, and he did not write 1 Timothy until around AD 64 and Titus around AD 62. Our tendency has always been to manufacture form and then try to squeeze the function into the already existing form. That's like a man who has a business idea coming up with an elaborate scheme to manage his business before he has sold or made anything. The way entrepreneurs work is to come up with a product or service and begin selling it. That's function. As the business grows, as the owner has a "tiger by the tail" so to speak, he then realizes he must have form in order to manage the growth he is experiencing.

We never find Paul's first move being to plant churches. He first went to an area and saw conversions, and from this new group of believers, churches began to be raised up. This means that evangelism must come first, asking God to give us disciples. From this, churches will come. It is like the great basketball coach John Wooden of UCLA. He always told his players to learn the fundamentals, to be in excellent physical condition, and to execute what they had learned, and to not worry about the score of the game. If they did what they were supposed to do then the winning would take care of itself.

Following this idea is the reality that churches will be

planted if we follow God's pattern. Evangelize, disciple the disciple makers, and churches will arise. This is precisely what Paul did. Observe his missionary journeys. He always went to the Jews first and, when they rejected him and his message, he then went to the Gentiles, all the while asking God to lead him to people who were open (God opened the heart of Lydia to hear the things spoke to hear by Paul). From there, a church was established in Lydia's household (Acts 16:14, 15).

International examples

Finally, the last thing we need to do is to learn from our brothers and sisters in the developing world. How is God growing the church so rapidly in Iran, India, and Afghanistan? Ordinary people, taxi drivers, schoolteachers, and government workers are following Jesus' model given to us in Luke 10. They are praying for God to open the hearts of people with whom they come in contact each day. They look for people whom He has chosen, who show interest in the gospel. They speak to them about their souls, and when their new friends call on the name of the Lord, they disciple them to maturity. That maturity begins the moment they are in an assembly of believers. The leaders do not wait for a year or more to make sure the people are ready to share Jesus. They get them going very quickly. Have you noticed how those baptized in the book of Acts were baptized immediately after their conversions? Why? Because baptism is an outward sign of an inward work. It is the means by which people identify with Christ in their new faith. Baptism is so familiar to us in the West that we tend to lose sight of its power. In the Muslim or Hindu world, baptism is a very big deal. It signals a departure from a former way of life, and this often costs those baptized their families, jobs, or sometimes their very lives. Our brethren in Hindu and Muslim lands are constantly praying for lost people who have needs, and when God hears their prayers, the unbeliever is often moved to consider the claims of the Lord. Shall we not take a play from the playbook of our brothers in other nations?

For the last twenty or more years, we have been hearing of Church Planting Movements or "Disciple Making Movements" in many developing nations, especially India, Nepal, Indonesia, Iran, Afghanistan, and many other Muslim countries, where amazing numbers of people are being converted. The whole movement is built on the concept of multiplication. Ordinary, non-ordained, and non-seminary trained men are taking seriously the task of discipling other disciple makers. These groups of believers do not worry about salaries, church buildings, or any of the traditional mores of western church life. They look for people of peace (Luke 10:5, 6), which means those who are open to the gospel. They preach Christ to them and encourage them to gather their *oikos* (Greek word for household) for a Bible study. In due time, large numbers of these households call on Christ to save them. But they are not content to stay in their small groups. Instead, they multiply, sometimes across three and four generations. There is clear evidence of entire Muslim and Hindu villages making Jesus their King and Savior through this method.

The evangelist has important and specific functions both within and outside the church. So why is the evangelist not utilized more? How many churches have actually used an evangelist, much less pushed for their ordination? How many churches give evangelists leadership in the church? How many use them for the specific task of equipping the church to do the work of evangelism? As the next chapter will demonstrate, there is a reason why Christ has given evangelists to the church—because there is a need for them.

What Is the Goal of the Evangelist?

If someone were to come to an evangelist and ask whether or not he has a fruitful ministry, how would the evangelist answer? What would be the first thing that came to mind? Conversions? Financial backing? Speaking engagements or conferences? How many times he's been arrested or mocked? How many cities or countries he has gone to with the gospel? All of these things can indeed be signs of a successful evangelistic ministry. But then again, in another sense, none of these things are signs of a successful ministry. Evangelists in the West had a significant influence on the culture for several centuries. They had been accustomed to "success" in some degree or another. Is the evangelist still successful if our evangelism sees little or no conversions? Is the evangelist still successful if he is unable to raise enough support to be full-time? If he never receives a speaking engagement? If he only evangelizes his neighborhood or city?[1]

---

1   Much of this chapter has been developed from a previous book, Ryan Denton, *Even if None: Reclaiming Biblical Evangelism* (San Francisco: FirstLove Publications, 2019).

Most evangelism ministries today seem driven by a desire to not offend anyone for the purpose of "winning souls" in a numerical sense. The desire for converts at any cost has not only pestered the church but also demonstrates a lack of understanding regarding biblical evangelism. When someone thinks the primary motivation of evangelism is to "save souls," methodologies will spring up that guarantee such an effect, however spurious or unbiblical they are—and however sincere the users of such methodologies may be. When such a motive is brought into a society that is unusually hardened to the gospel, the natural alternative is to find ways to make the gospel and evangelism more pleasing to the lost, even if it means watering down the gospel for the sake of kindness and being inoffensive, thinking that this is the magical concoction for saving people. But the goal of the evangelist is not primarily to win souls, although he should pray and preach to that effect.

Consider, for instance, that many missions and church planting organizations in the West will pull support unless a certain quota of members or conversions is met after a specific period of time. It goes without saying that this will influence the church planter or evangelist to accommodate doctrine and church polity to those who would otherwise never go to church. This approach assumes that church growth and conversion is somehow directly related to the church planter or evangelist. It assumes that church growth and conversion is the work of man.

The Bible teaches that God gives the increase, not man (1 Cor. 3:6), and that salvation is of the Lord (Psalm 3:8), which is why the Scriptures nowhere imply that church leaders or Christians should set numerical goals for church growth. Noah, Isaiah, and even Paul would have been seen as "unsuccessful" by such standards, despite their unquestionable faithfulness and care for people's souls. The same is true of William Carey or Adoniram Judson, missionaries to India who both labored for almost a decade before seeing one convert. Will Metzger concurs, noting that "the question of whether or not we are evangelizing cannot be settled by counting the number of converts. In that case, many faithful missionaries who have seen no converts from years of labor would have to be rebuked for lack of witnessing."[2] It is bad enough that the land is spiritually hardened. But now those called to evangelize in such an environment must either submit to the "success-driven" Evangelicalism through manipulations and a watered-down gospel or give an account for why they are so "unsuccessful."

This is what we see today when it comes to evangelism. There is a frantic hurry "to get members into the church" or to have an "apparatus for decisions." There is a drive to preach "come forward" instead of "repent and believe." When evangelizing outside the church, there is a passion to see some kind of tangible fruit for the purpose of telling others that x-number of people accepted Jesus. Of course, we desire to see people converted, but what is driving these desires to see, or perhaps better put, *force* results? Do we do it for "the one"? And if so, what if "the one" never comes? What if we never see salvific fruit? Do we accommodate the message? Do we present a gospel easier to accept or more "effective" in the realm of salvific numbers? Do we quit evangelizing?

Most Christians today are likely to define evangelism as something that yields results in the sphere of salvation or church growth. These things are unlikely to occur without evangelism taking place, but there is tremendous danger here. Numerical yields of salvation and church growth should never be the aim of evangelism or ministry in general. Joel Osteen, Jehovah's Witnesses, and The Church of Jesus Christ of Latter-Day Saints can grow a "church" numerically and get many "converts." But this is no sign of doing it biblically.

So, what is the goal of the evangelist? It is to be faithful in proclaiming the gospel. It is to be faithful in praying for conversions. It is to be faithful in equipping the saints to do

---

2   Will Metzger, *Tell the Truth* (Downers Grove, IL: InterVarsity, 1981), 56.

evangelism. Glorifying God through our faithfulness should be the aim, leaving salvation and church growth up to the Lord. The New Testament rarely defines evangelism through the lens of results, but rather as conveying the gospel to unbelievers, which includes the call to repent and believe, as well as a clear articulation of what it means to "count the cost" of following Christ. This is why Morton H. Smith in *Reformed Evangelism* says that evangelism is simply "to set forth the good news."[3] He makes the observation that "sometimes we think of evangelism as including the result... but evangelism should not be defined in terms of the results, rather, it should be defined in terms of the activity of setting forth the good news itself."[4] Again, this is not to say that conversions are unimportant. It is not to say that our motive for evangelizing is irrelevant. It is not to say that evangelism should be without urgency or passion. But it is to point out that evangelism is sharing the gospel with the lost, period, and that this must be the aim of the evangelist.

J. I. Packer claims that the confusion about "present-day debates" regarding evangelism can be attributed to "our widespread and persistent habit of defining evangelism in terms, not of a message delivered, but of an effect produced in our hearers."[5] Some have pointed out that a biblical view of evangelism is one of the marks of a healthy church. This would imply that a church with a contrary view of evangelism would be unhealthy. So, what is an example of an unbiblical view of evangelism? "One of the most common and dangerous mistakes is to confuse the results of evangelism with evangelism itself. This may be the most subtle of the misunderstandings. Evangelism must not be confused with the fruit of evangelism."[6]

Such statements are as tragic as they are shocking. When it

---

3   Morton H. Smith, *Reformed Evangelism* (Clinton, MS: Multi-Communication Ministries, 1975), 4.

4   Smith, *Reformed Evangelism*, 4.

5   J. I. Packer, *Evangelism and the Sovereignty of God* (Downers Grove, IL: InterVarsity Press, 1961), 41.

6   Mark Dever, *Nine Marks of a Healthy Church* (Wheaton, IL: Crossway, 2000), 134.

comes to conversion, the most difficult area of all Christianity to evaluate, we must leave such numbering to God, who alone "looks on the heart" (1 Sam. 16:7) and who alone grants faith to the unbeliever. Since the Lord is the author of Scripture, the Bible can use phrases, such as "and there were added that day about three thousand souls" and "the number of the men came to about five thousand."[7] But even here we see that nothing like an official count took place, since in both places the phrase "about" is used, which implies an estimation. This is much different than what is usually seen in modern Christianity today.

This is why posting numbers of "salvations" or baptisms was not a typical practice of our forefathers, including Spurgeon, Edwards, and Whitefield, all of whom saw large numeric success from their evangelism. They understood biblical conversion well enough to know it is hazardous to publish such statistics considering the spurious nature of "professions" in general. Spurgeon was especially opposed to the publication of "numbers" regarding professions and baptisms:

> What mean these dispatches from the battlefield? 'Last night 14 souls were under conviction, 15 were justified, and 8 received full sanctification.' I am weary of these public braggings, this counting of unhatched chickens, this exhibition of doubtful spoils. Lay aside such numberings of the people, such idle pretense of certifying in half a minute that which will need the testing of a lifetime.[8]

This is not to say that external signs are useless when it comes to evaluating whether or not a person is converted. In a sense, they are all we have to go by. Rather, it is to say that external signs should not be the aim of evangelism. Communicating the gospel clearly and without compromise should be the aim,

---

7 Acts 2:41, Acts 4:4

8 Iain H. Murray, *Revival & Revivalism* (Carlisle, PA: The Banner of Truth Trust, 1994), 408.

regardless of the results or external signs. Martyn Lloyd-Jones rightly claims that the supreme object of evangelism is to glorify God, not to save souls, and that the motivation for evangelism is a zeal for God, primarily, and a love for others, secondarily.[9]

The Bible also shows that evangelism will often result in a gospel call that is not efficacious, which is especially important to remember for Christians living in the West. This is presupposed when Christ says, "He that believes and is baptized shall be saved, but he that disbelieves shall be condemned" (Mark 16:15-16). The parable of the marriage feast in Matthew 22:2-14 concludes that "many are called, but few chosen." The Scriptures nowhere imply that, considering how often there is little to no success when evangelizing, we should try some other method or that it is not evangelism. Ernest C. Reisinger goes a step further when he points out that even damnation is a result of evangelism, and hence it is effective even when none are saved: "There are two results: (1) '...he that believeth and is baptized shall be saved.' (2) '...he that believeth not shall be damned.' Salvation is one result, and damnation is another result."[10] One paragraph later, he states,

> When the biblical gospel is preached, there will be results, and God will be glorified...His justice, holiness, and righteousness will be glorified in the damnation of those who believe not. Many modern preachers do not like even to mention this aspect of the results, but it is clear in the Bible. When God reveals His mercy, He always reveals His judgment, and the Bible makes this very clear.

This means that evangelism is always effective, regardless of how a person responds, since the Lord is glorified either way. This is also why we can be truthful and bold about making

---

9   D. Martyn Lloyd-Jones, *The Presentation of the Gospel* (London: Inter-Varsity Fellowship, 1949), pp. 6-7.

10   Ernest C. Reisinger, *Today's Evangelism* (Philipsburg, NJ: Craig Press, 1982), 11.

sure the unsaved know the cost of following Christ, which was His own method of dealing with men's souls. Martyn Lloyd-Jones notes: "Go through the ministry of our Lord Himself and you cannot but get the impression that at times, far from pressing people to follow Him and decide for Him, He put great obstacles in their way. He said in effect: 'Do you realize what you are doing? Have you counted the cost?'"[11] Another writer points to the Rich Young Ruler as an example: "Concern for the nobleman's soul was not the supreme motive that moved Christ to witness to this sinner. Running even deeper within His breast was a love of God. Though induced by a desire to save men, Christ was primarily motivated by a longing to glorify His Father."[12] Because Christ's motive was the glory of God, not "the one," He was able to communicate the demands of the biblical gospel, however impossible they would be to accept.

The following are verbs used in the Acts of the Apostles to describe the work of evangelism: to testify (Acts 2:40), to proclaim (Acts 4:2), to preach the gospel (Acts 5:42), to herald (Acts 8:5), to teach (Acts 4:2), to argue (Acts 17:2), to dispute (Acts 9:29), to confound (Acts 9:22), to prove (Acts 17:3), to confute powerfully (Acts 18:28), to persuade (Acts 17:4).[13] On the contrary, phrases not used or implied in the Acts of the Apostles to describe evangelism would include building bridges, establishing common ground, "friendship evangelism," or entertaining the lost. Ironically, there is also no mention of "love" in the Acts of the Apostles.[14]

Even biblical Christians can be influenced by unbiblical methods that neuter the offense of the cross. Even the Reformed

---

11 D. Martyn Lloyd-Jones, *Studies in the Sermon on the Mount* (Grand Rapids: W. B. Eerdman's, 1984), 207.

12 Walter J. Chantry, *Today's Gospel* (Carlisle, PA: The Banner of Truth, 1970), 23.

13 John Stott, *Christian Mission in the Modern World* (Downers Grove, IL: InterVarsity Press, 2008), 60.

14 Even though, of course, the chief motivation of evangelism was love for God and man.

church has been influenced into thinking numbers or "salvific fruit" is the main catalyst for evangelism. If we are not seeing people saved or filling our churches, we have come to believe we are "ineffective" and should try something else. If someone is upset with us or calls us narrow-minded or bigoted when evangelizing, we are tempted to go about evangelism in a different, softer manner. This is not to say that we should be obnoxious or profane when evangelizing. On the contrary, we should be respectful. Our genuine concern for the lost should be evident to all men. We should exude love for our hearers. But it is to say that our evangelism should not become man-centered or pragmatic just because it does not see conversions.

Will Metzger describes the gospel as "a word message announcing good news. The key Greek words connected to the gospel refer to communication by words, talk, speech."[15] He also notes that "verbal communication (of the gospel) was the means by which the gospel spread."[16] This is why anything that makes the gospel secondary is unbiblical. "The key to biblical evangelism is not strategy or technique. It is not primarily about style, methodology, or programs and pragmatics. The first and preeminent concern in all our evangelistic efforts must be the gospel."[17]

This method of hearing the gospel is found throughout the Scriptures. Writing to the Romans, Paul says, "So then faith comes by hearing, and hearing by the word of God" (Rom. 10:17). When writing to the Thessalonians, he says, "For this reason we also thank God without ceasing, because when you received the word of God which you heard from us, you welcomed it not as the word of men, but as it is in truth, the word of God, which also effectively works in you who believe" (1 Thes. 2:13). And again, when writing to the Galatians, Paul

---

15   Will Metzger, *Tell the Truth* (Downers Grove, IL: InterVarsity, 1981), 32.

16   Metzger, *Tell the Truth*, 32.

17   John MacArthur and Jesse Johnson, "Rediscovering Biblical Evangelism," *Evangelism* (Nashville, TN: Thomas Nelson, 2011), viii-ix.

says, "Did you receive the Spirit by the works of the Law, or by hearing with faith" (Gal. 3:2)? To the Ephesians he says, "In Him you also trusted, after you heard the word of truth, the gospel of your salvation" (Eph. 1:13). This is where biblical evangelism comes in: "How then shall they call on Him in whom they have not believed? And how shall they believe in Him of whom they have not heard? And how shall they hear without a preacher?" (Rom. 10:14).

The *Belgic Confession* says something similar in Article XXIV: "We believe that this true faith, being wrought in man by the hearing of the Word of God and the operation of the Holy Ghost, doth regenerate and make him a new man, causing him to live a new life, and freeing him from the bondage of sin." Faith is wrought in man through the hearing of the gospel and the effectual application of it by the Holy Spirit. It is that simple. Throughout church history, beginning in Adam's day, the Holy Spirit applying the proclamation of the Word of God is what converts the elect. The *Second London Baptist Confession* states that "the gospel is the only outward means of revealing Christ and saving grace, and it is abundantly sufficient for that purpose."[18] This sentence encapsulates everything that needs to be said regarding biblical evangelism, which is simply revealing Christ's "saving grace" to the lost. Such an approach is certain to be "abundantly sufficient," regardless of salvific results, which is the point that needs to be emphasized. Gordon H. Clark describes evangelism as simply "the exposition of the Scripture. God will do the regenerating."[19]

This is not to say that evangelism can only be done through auditory proclamation, as opposed to some form of written medium. Any time the content of the gospel is communicated to an unbeliever, whether through a gospel tract, the Bible,

---

18 2LBC 20:4

19 Gordon H. Clark, *Today's Evangelism: Counterfeit or Genuine?* (Unicoi, TN: The Trinity Foundation, 1990), 274.

or something else, evangelism is happening. But it does mean words are necessary, unlike what we see in many ministries today, where showing the gospel is equated with sharing it:

> Some people might say, 'We don't have to say anything about the gospel. Our lifestyle will say it all.' Others might quote the words of that old song, 'They will know we are Christians by our love.' Still others quote the words often wrongly attributed to Francis of Assisi (1181/82-1226), 'Preach the gospel at all times—if necessary, use words.' But we ought to look carefully again at Acts 11 to see what the church did there. Believers spoke of the wonderful grace of God in Christ...They told people with words the good news about the Lord Jesus.[20]

The biblical evangelist is the one who gets the gospel to the lost. That should be his aim. Any other "method" can be contributed to a lack of faith in the gospel and a disbelief in the sufficiency of the Bible, which alone should be our guide for how to "do" evangelism. "Our evangelism must be based upon a dependence on the Lord. Our hope of results must be in Him, not in man's will or in any other faculty of our hearer. But it pleases God to raise dead sinners through the foolishness of gospel preaching."[21]

God Converts, Not Man

The goal of evangelism is the glory of God, which is done every time we get the gospel to the lost. The goal of evangelism is not to save them, since salvation is of the Lord, not the preacher: "God never laid it upon thee to convert those he sends thee to. No, to publish the gospel is thy duty."[22]

---

20 Wes Bredenhof, *To Win Our Neighbors for Christ* (Grand Rapids, MI: Reformation Heritage Books, 2012), 48.

21 Chantry, *Today's Gospel*, 86.

22 William Gurnall, *The Christian in Complete Armour* (1662; reprint London: Banner of Truth Trust, 1964), 574.

This is why anything cute or silly or wise according to this world will only distract from the simple message of the cross. J. I. Packer deals with this problem effectively when he says, "If we regard our job, not simply to present Christ, but actually to produce converts...our approach to evangelism would become pragmatic and calculating. Techniques would become ends in themselves."[23] Plain gospel proclamation must be the goal of evangelism. This could include while at a church pizza party or some kind of building project, for example, so long as the gospel is being clearly communicated. It could also include a conversation at work, open air preaching, or a gospel tract left with a person at a restaurant. It would also include while at home with family. Packer notes, "The way to tell whether in fact you are evangelizing is not to ask whether conversions are known to have resulted from your witness. It is to ask whether you are faithfully making known the gospel message."[24] George W. Robertson agrees in his booklet, *What is Evangelism?*: "The Bible never hints that the herald is the converter. Persuasion or conversion is possible only when the Spirit removes 'a heart of stone' and replaces it with a 'heart of flesh' (Ezek. 36:26) and 'opens' it to receive the free offer of grace" (Acts 16:40).[25] Conversion is something that no human could ever do for another human. But what we are called to do is share the gospel, which the Lord shows to be the proper method for evangelism.

We must declare the gospel to all the world, including "that all people everywhere should repent" (Acts 17:30). We must wrestle with men's souls, pleading they be reconciled to God through Jesus Christ (1 Cor. 5:20). We must tell men to "choose this day whom you will serve" (Josh. 24:15), though the effectual call of the gospel is a work of God alone. God is sovereign

---

23 J. I. Packer, *Evangelism and the Sovereignty of God* (Downers Grove, IL: InterVarsity Press, 1961), 122.

24 Packer, *Evangelism and the Sovereignty of God*, 41.

25 George W. Robertson, *What is Evangelism?* (Phillipsburg, NJ: P&R, 2013), 6.

in all things, especially salvation, even though He condescends to use "the foolishness of preaching to save them that believe" (1 Cor. 1:21). We must preach the cross and resurrection. We must preach repentance and faith in Christ, bidding sinners to come to Him, knowing that all the while salvation is a gift of God: "Can the Ethiopian change his skin or the leopard its spots? Then may you also do good who are accustomed to do evil" (Jer. 13:23).

Biblical evangelism is getting the Word of God to the people for the sake of God's glory, not "the one." This is not to say that "the one" does not matter. It is not to say that people are irrelevant when it comes to evangelism. On the contrary, our love for our neighbor should also be a catalyst, especially when it comes to our tone, approach, and urgency. But our primary aim is God's glory, which abounds all the more any time we speak of Christ. Whether at work, a college campus, downtown, at an abortion clinic, on the phone with a relative, or at home with our family, get the gospel to the lost. What happens next is up to God. John MacArthur writes, "Evangelism is a privileged calling. We do what we can to spread the gospel wherever we are able. Then we go home and go to sleep. If we have worked hard we can sleep well, knowing, as the farmer did, that the growth does not depend on us."[26]

This was the view not only of the Apostles, but the Reformers and Puritans as well. Louis Berkhof notes that "according to Calvin the gospel call is not in itself effective but is made efficacious by the operation of the Holy Spirit, when He savingly applies the Word to the heart of man; and it is so applied only in the hearts and lives of the elect. Thus, the salvation of man remains the work of God from the very beginning."[27]

Since God is sovereign in salvation and man incapable of being "born-again" apart from God's regenerating grace, the

---

26 John MacArthur, "Theology of Sleep," *Evangelism* (Nashville, TN: Thomas Nelson, 2011), 17.

27 Louis Berkhof, *Systematic Theology* (Carlisle, PA: The Banner of Truth, 1958), 459.

Christian can go out in total dependence on God. He will be liberated from the burden of "saying the right thing" or the fear he will say "the wrong thing." He cannot push people "further" away from God. People whose minds are set on the flesh are "hostile to God" (Rom. 8:7) and can't be "pushed" any further than they already are. Since evangelism is not about producing converts but rather being faithful in delivering the gospel, the mark of "successful" evangelism cannot be interpreted by how many persons are saved. This allows the Christian to focus on sharing the content of the gospel, not his own devices. Even if the "gospel chariot" returns "blurred and reproached, wearing the marks of hell's spite," the laborer can rejoice, knowing that only God can replace "a heart of stone" with "a heart of flesh" (Ezek. 36:26), but he himself has been faithful to proclaim the gospel.

This is not to say that we are satisfied if no one is saved, but rather that God is glorified through the proclamation of the gospel, regardless of the results. John MacArthur points out the great advantage of God's sovereignty when evangelizing: "We know when we witness or preach that God has His chosen ones who will respond positively, and that should encourage us to be faithful. Election is not an excuse for inactivity. Those who think they can remain idle and leave it to God to save the elect through some mystical means do not understand the Scriptures."[28]

---

28   John MacArthur, *Ashamed of the Gospel* (Wheaton, IL: Crossway Books, 1993), 180.

How to Discern if Someone Is an Evangelist

Now that we have seen that evangelists are needed in the church today, how do we know who the evangelists are? How would someone go about deciding whether or not he was being called to be an evangelist? Is it whether or not converts are made through his ministry? Whether or not he is good at evangelizing? Whether or not he is a passionate preacher? You get the drift.

None of the above criteria are wrong, necessarily, but they are not exactly correct, either. For instance, if converts were a criterion, people like Hudson Taylor, Isaiah the prophet, and even Jesus would not qualify. It is true that the evangelist will see conversions take place, but there is more to it than this. Many times, what we believe are converts actually turn out to be rotten fruit. Jesus warns of this in the parable of the sower (Mark 4:1-20). Other times, people may be saved through our evangelism even if we never know about it. Stories abound of people being converted by a particular sermon or gospel presentation long after the event takes place. Also, being gifted at evangelism is important, as we will see, but most of the time a person just starting out as an evangelist is not "good" at it yet. He will still be very rough around the edges. Also, people who are not evangelists in the official sense can still be very effective at evangelizing. We know many women who are gifted at sharing the gospel, but they would not qualify for the office of evangelist (1 Tim. 2:12; 1 Tim. 3). Passion when preaching can be helpful, but it is not everything. Many heretics are passionate preachers. Many orthodox preachers who are not evangelists in the official sense of the word are passionate preachers. So how do you know whether or not you are an evangelist?

Evangelists desire to evangelize

The first thing to look for in an evangelist is a desire to do the work. When God calls a person to a ministry, they will be burdened about seeing it through. When an evangelist is being called by God, he will begin to think about ways to evangelize. He will consider methods and places to evangelize. His mind will be occupied with the idea of evangelism, even if he has yet to do much of it. This is different from other Christians. Every Christian is called to evangelize, and every Christian will desire to do it, but not every Christian has a burning obsession to do it. Not every Christian will be consumed by the topic.

From here, the evangelist will begin to evangelize. Again, every Christian is called to take this step, but there is something different about the way an evangelist goes about it. Whether open air preaching or one-on-one conversation, the evangelist will relish any opportunity to proclaim the things of God to the lost. It doesn't mean the evangelist will find every situation to be easy or comfortable. Like Paul the Apostle, there will be much fear and trembling. But the fire in the bones will overcome any obstacle. The evangelist will use every free moment he has to either evangelize or study for the sake of being a better evangelist. It will be his passion. It will be his life's purpose. Over time, the evangelist will become better at evangelizing, but it doesn't mean he ever gets to the point where he no longer relies on the Lord. This is what is called the internal call. The evangelist is driven to spend and be spent in the work of evangelism.

Others will notice this gift for evangelism

But internal calls are subjective and not always correct. Today, many women will say they have a call to preach or teach, even to other men. But we know this can't be true since the Scriptures forbid women preaching and teaching. God would not call someone to do something that He expressly forbids. The same can be true in the case of someone believing they are an evangelist. This is the importance of an external call.

Ideally, the church will recognize individuals who are being called by God to be an evangelist. This can be tricky, of course, since many churches may be reluctant to call anyone to the office of evangelist. But at the very least, most churches will acknowledge if a person has the call or gift to evangelize, and hopefully they will help cultivate this gift. This is an important step. Even though we have new hearts as Christians, we still have the tendency to think better of ourselves than we ought. We still have the tendency to be led away into deception, especially when it pertains to our own abilities. Spurgeon recognized that a person who isn't a good preacher isn't being called to preach, regardless of how desirous he is to do it.[1] Again, think of how many women preach or teach to men simply because they feel like they should. The external call provides guardrails both for us and those around us, assuming that the "external" part of the external call is made up of godly, biblical Christians who will tell the truth to the person trying to decide if they are an evangelist. We must remember that the work is more important than

---

1   Lectures to My Students

us. We must put aside our feelings and desires and seek true, honest, and oftentimes difficult council from godly persons.

Only mature men are qualified to be evangelists

Since it continues to come up, when it comes to the evangelist, only men are qualified to hold the office. Women can be very effective at evangelism. Every Christian woman should be evangelizing. But in an official capacity, women are not qualified to hold the office. There are no precedents in the New Testament of women serving as evangelists in any official capacity. Also, because part of the task of the office of evangelist is to teach others how to evangelize, women are barred from the role since they are not to teach nor have authority over men in any kind of official way (1 Tim. 2:12). Naturally, this may be offensive to a culture steeped in feminism, but this is God's pattern for ordering His church. Women and men are equal in dignity, value and worth because both women and men are made in the image of God. But women and men have different roles, functions and even gifts, and problems arise when such roles and functions begin to be either blended or switched.

Also, the evangelist should be a mature Christian if he is to hold the office of evangelist. Ideally, the evangelist will be an elder in his church and so will satisfy the requirements for this role in 1 Timothy 3 and Titus 1. Despite the reluctance of some churches to recognize or ordain an evangelist as an elder, the evangelist is someone should still be a mature Christian. The reasons for this are both theological and practical. Theologically, as we have seen, the evangelist is lumped together in the same passage as the pastor and teacher, and who would dare say a pastor or teacher does not need to satisfy the requirements of 1 Timothy 3 and Titus 1? Who would dare say an immature Christian could ably discharge the duties of a pastor or teacher? Why would we assume it to be different when it comes to the evangelist? The evangelist especially needs to be someone who is mature and able to teach. Practically speaking, unlike the pastor and teacher, the evangelist will regularly be mixing with lost people. He will be around their language and worldview. He will be exposed to certain thinking patterns and temptations that pastors and teachers are largely insulated from. The evangelist must be mature. He must be stable.

Perseverance a hallmark of the evangelist

Lastly, the evangelist will persevere in the work if he is truly called by God. The evangelist's work is arguably the most difficult of all ministries. This is not to downplay the difficulty of pastoring and teaching, nor is it to say that the evangelist is somehow superior to the rest of the church officers. It is simply to warn anyone attempting to pursue the call of an evangelist to be prepared for the world, the church, and even family to come against him. The role of the evangelist is in large part to bring the gospel to people who will be unthankful and unbelieving. It is to engage people who think the evangelist and the message are foolish. In the church, the evangelist will be misunderstood. He won't have many conferences that cater to his ministry. Not many books will be written about his calling. Not many people will be interested in his zeal to save souls.

The culture in the West is not "Christian." Such a statement should not be shocking. The cultures in most parts of the world are also not Christian. But for evangelists who live in other parts of the world, severe persecution has long been underway, including martyrdom. The same is on the horizon for Western evangelists. There is already an increase of arrests and lawsuits against evangelists, but it is still mild compared to most of the world and even to what we see in church history. Evangelists must be prepared to face persecution both physically and financially. That does not mean that evangelists have to go looking for trouble. It is not to say that evangelists should have a type of martyr complex. It is to say that faithful evangelists, because they are on the front lines, will be the first to experience backlash from their culture. They will be the first Christians to see certain trends and patterns in secular society's thinking and behavior. Any evangelist can attest to how troubling such insights can be, especially if no one else is aware of it yet. For instance, the Marxism and atheism that is gripping the United States today could be seen long ago by anyone ministering on college campuses. The trend against free speech, so apparent today, was recognized by evangelists decades ago whenever they went out to share Christ with the lost, especially in the open air. But an evangelist will be one who endures in his call.

Jesus talks about a rocky-soil person who, though he receives the word "with joy," endures until "tribulation or persecution arises on account of the word," which then causes him to "fall away" (Mat. 13:20-21). Although the parable is speaking about biblical conversion, it provides a helpful illustration for what happens to many supposed evangelists, as well. They begin well. They are excited to do the work. They are passionate about what it entails. But over time, they lose interest. They lose hunger. They lose desire. The pushback from the world, the church, and family become too much. They fall away from the call. They get comfortable. They are no longer as eager to see people saved or train Christians to evangelize. As with any other calling, there can be a certain romanticism involved about evangelism which, once the path is taken, suddenly becomes less romantic. It becomes less exciting.

The evangelist must not be surprised by the pushback, however. The evangelist must not go into this work with false hopes. The cross of Christ has always been an offense to mankind, but the evangelist's job is to share it anyways. Fiery trials will come against the one who proclaims the gospel to the lost, especially on a regular basis. The evangelist must set his face like flint and plow on for the sake of his King. He must declare what "great things the Lord hath done" (Mark 5:19). There is a reason Paul was lashed 195 times, stoned once, beaten with rods on three different occasions, and was in danger from

Jews, Gentiles, and false believers (2 Cor. 11:24–26). He opened his mouth about Christ in public and proclaimed the only way to God. The evangelist must pray for strength to do the same. Recall the words of Jesus during His last supper with the disciples:

> "If the world hates you, you know that it hated me before it hated you. If you were of the world, the world would love his own: but because you are not of the world, but I have chosen you out of the world, therefore the world hates you. Remember the word that I said unto you, 'The servant is not greater than his lord.' If they have persecuted me, they will also persecute you; if they have kept my saying, they will keep yours also" (John 15:18-20).

The evangelist is promised suffering and the hatred of the world. More than this, and worst of all, the church or his family may even come against him. His flesh will come against him. The devil will come against him. But he must believe that the Lamb is worthy to suffer for and go on anyway.

The key to doing the work of an evangelist is the necessity of staying at it, of persevering, no matter what the response of people may be. Perseverance with people in pursuit of their salvation is an absolute necessity. Rarely do people become believers the first time they hear the gospel. This is hard work.

I remember a few years ago taking several people out to evangelize door-to-door. The weather was very hot and humid. After two hours of this on a Saturday morning, we all came back to the church for a de-briefing. All of us were soaked with sweat. I said to the men:

> "We made lots of great contacts this morning and there is much you can build upon for the future. You can see, however, that this is really hard work. You will need to persevere. This is not for the faint of heart or those who lack discipline. This work will frustrate and exhaust you,

but it will also thrill and humble you as you see God, usually over a period of time, bring forth the fruit of repentance in the salvation of people."

Here's the question—will you commit to this work of evangelistic outreach in your community? How can you very specifically get started? List a thing or two you can do, find a few people to join you and the evangelists God has given you, and just do it. Just execute your plan and see what God does with it over a one- or two-year period. A mature man who desires to do the work of an evangelist, who is good at the work of evangelism, who has received confirmation from others about his work as an evangelist, and who perseveres in the work despite all obstacles can be confident that he has been called by God as an evangelist. It may be one of the most difficult ministries a man can have, but it is also the most rewarding, both in this life and for the life to come.

Advice for Evangelists

Advice for Evangelists—
Be Absorbed in the Work

We all know that many ministers and evangelists have fallen prey to the schemes of the world, the flesh, and the devil and made shipwreck of their faith and family, not to mention bringing great shame to the work of Christ and His church. This chapter is an attempt to safeguard against such tragedies. We need to look at some Biblical data on the topic. From there we will address some of the pitfalls specifically related to evangelistic ministry. Finally, we will deal very practically with the remedy which can keep us on the straight and narrow path which leads to fruitful, long-lasting, and God-honoring ministry.

Faithfulness in ministry begins with the heart

First, let's take a look at what the Scriptures have to say about maintaining biblical fidelity in our ministries. Proverbs 4:23 exhorts us to watch over our hearts with all diligence, for from them flow the springs of life. Let's briefly break this down. By *hearts* the writer means the very center of our being, the essence of who we are as human beings made in the image of God. The unbeliever has a rebellious heart, what Psalm 58 calls a cobra heart. Psalm 51 says that we were conceived in sin and brought forth in iniquity. Jeremiah 17 says that the unbeliever's heart is deceitful and above all desperately wicked. The unbeliever hates God and loves sin. He is enslaved to the devil. Jesus says that the unbeliever is a child of the devil. John tells us that the whole unbelieving world lies in the hands of the evil one. The unbeliever can never please God. He is alienated from God. He is hostile in his mind toward Him. He is engaged in evil deeds all his days. Now, he is not necessarily as bad as he could be. The Scriptures acknowledge what theologians call "common grace." The vestiges of God's image remain to a greater or lesser degree in the heart of every unregenerate person. Nonetheless, he hates God. He is like a spitting cobra we find in East Africa. He spits out venom to God and people.

The Christian man, however, is different. God has taken out his heart of stone and given him a heart of flesh. He is born-again to a living hope through the resurrection of Jesus Christ from the dead. He is born from above. He is indwelt by the Holy Spirit. He has been transformed on the inside. His heart is no longer unregenerate or corrupt. The old has passed away and the new has come. In the very essence of his being, due to his new heart, his bent is to love and serve God. He still, however, battles indwelling sin, the old man, and the flesh. Indwelling sin is the propensity of everyone, including believers, to move away from God and toward disobedience. Paul told the Romans that in him, that is in his flesh, dwells no good thing. The very thing he wished to do, he did not do, and the thing he hated to do, he did. The old man, what you were in Adam before your con-version, how you acted, thought, and spoke as an unbeliever, still hinders you. In the believer the flesh is constantly being weakened through the sanctifying work of the Spirit, but the old man and the flesh continue to plague the believer until the day he dies. And indwelling sin is still very much present in the believer as well.

So the author of Proverbs tells us to watch over our hearts, the very essence of who we are. This is true of the Christian. What does it mean to "watch over our hearts?" To watch over something is to guard it, to protect it, to be a good steward of it. Paul instructs the elders of the church at Ephesus to be on guard for themselves and for the flock over which the Holy Spirit made them overseers. Why? Because savage wolves are always coming into the church to lead us astray from the truth. We are told to watch over our hearts with diligence. The opposite of diligence is negligence. If you plant a garden in the spring and do nothing to cultivate the garden and get the weeds out of it, then the weeds will take over in short order and you will have very little yield from your garden. To be negligent is to do nothing to stop the natural inclination we all have toward the ruin of our souls.

On the other hand, to be diligent is to be proactive, to be disciplined, to take matters into our hands and to do something about the declension toward which we all naturally move. Think of the comptroller of a company. His job is to manage the money of the business, to make sure expenditures are in line with the goals of the business. Failure here could lead to financial ruin. The Christian is exhorted to watch over, to guard in a very disciplined and diligent manner, the essence of who he is. He is to be ruthless. He is not to allow anything to enter his mind, his eye gate, or his ear gate which could jeopardize his walk with God. This is a constant command the believer must obey every day of his Christian life. He can never "take a vacation" from his duty.

Why? Why is this necessary? Because from the heart flow the springs of life. Think of a lake near your house. Perhaps it is spring fed. An aquifer surfaces and begins to fill up the surrounding low lying property. Soon, a lake forms, and the underwater river continues to send water to the surface through the spring and constantly supplies the lake with water. And then life springs up in the lake. It is filled with fish and ducks which came to the lake to eat and live.

The heart of man is the spring from which all of man's life comes. His heart effects his speech. A pure heart speaks the truth in love and always edifies. Such speech is gracious, seasoned as if it were with salt. An impure heart, on the other hand, brings forth coarse, ungodly, vile, and contemptible speech. One way you can always discern the condition of your heart is to listen to what you are saying and how you are saying it. But the heart also reveals the condition of one's mind and actions. Lustful, deceitful, bitter, and angry thoughts make clear the heart condition of any man. When these are present, then we can be sure that he is not where he needs to be. This man needs to examine his heart and repent. The same is true with his actions. A vile heart leads to vile thoughts, vile affections, vile speech, and eventually vile actions. We never sin in a vacuum. There are decisions we make daily which move us away from God or toward God. So, how are you doing with your heart? Are you being negligent? What are you watching on your iPhone? What are you reading? What kind of music do you listen to? You are either improving or declining.

Be absorbed in the work

Another passage of Scripture which ought to receive our attention is Paul's exhortation to young Timothy:

> Do not neglect the spiritual gift within you, which was granted to you through words of prophecy with the laying on of hands by the council of elders. Take pains with these things; be absorbed in them, so that your progress will be evident to all. Pay close attention to yourself and to the teaching; persevere in these things, for as you do this you will save both yourself and those who hear you, (1 Tim. 4:14-16).

Paul was constantly exhorting Timothy to suffer hardship as a good soldier of Jesus Christ. He told Timothy not to become entangled with the world; to compete as an athlete according to the rules; to be diligent to present himself approved of God; not to wrangle about words, which is unprofitable and leads to ungodliness, along with many other similar commands.

Most of you reading this book have a keen interest in ministry in general and evangelistic ministry in particular. You may be an evangelist, gifted, called, and equipped by the Holy Spirit to engage with people on the streets of our cities in order to preach Christ to them. Therefore, this exhortation from Paul to Timothy is most appropriate for your serious consideration. If you are an evangelist, then do not neglect this spiritual gift which has come to you from God. The apostles were able to bestow gifts on men in order for them to expand the work of Christ's kingdom. The Holy Spirit has gifted and called you. Do not neglect that gift. So, how might you be guilty of neglecting this evangelistic gift God has given you? To neglect something is to not use it. You may be a carpenter, for example, and neglect to use a certain saw for the project. That's just stupid. Why would you not use the proper tool? By design it is to make your work more effectual and easy. If you are not out regularly preaching the gospel on the streets or seeking to engage people in your community one-on-one with the gospel, then you are neglecting this gift. If you have learned to speak Spanish but neglect using your newfound skill, then you very quickly will lose what you earlier had. This gift is from God. Use it or lose it.

Paul goes on to tell Timothy to take great pains with these things. He is to work hard, to be diligent, like an athlete in the weight room training daily to get stronger. An athlete can very quickly lose his top notch physical conditioning with only a few days of neglect. I remember when I was in high school playing basketball. Our coach really ran us a lot in order for us to be top physical condition. Back in those days we had no games or practices for about ten days during the Christmas holidays. The first day of practice after ten days of lying around and eating turkey and pumpkin pie was brutal. We were out of shape. We were sucking wind big time. In a much greater way, our failure to use and hone the gift of evangelism will mean that we will lose what gains we had earlier made.

Paul goes further to tell Timothy that he is to be absorbed in them. In other words, a mere casual approach at working to develop and not neglect this spiritual gift will never do. We are called to be absorbed in this pursuit. We are to be serious, single-minded, not moved away from the task at hand. I remember watching one of our grandchildren work on the Lego set we gave him for Christmas. He was five years old at the time and he put himself in the corner of his living room and proceeded to spend the next three hours nonstop working on the project. His brothers were running around the house playing but he was locked in. He could not be moved from his task. He blocked out all distractions. He was absorbed in finishing the Lego set.

Are you absorbed in the work of evangelism? Are you dedicated to becoming the best evangelist you can possibly be? What exactly does it look like to be absorbed in the work of honing your evangelistic gift? Among other things, it means to work at it regularly. You should preach every opportunity you can get. You should make every effort to evangelize whenever God opens a door. Practice your preaching. I remember going into a vacant room at a church I worked at before going to seminary and preaching sermons to the empty chairs.

Paul promises Timothy that if he does so then his progress will be evident to all. On the one hand, preaching is like any other skill. You never stand still. You are always improving or digressing. The more you practice it and gain feedback from others, the more you will develop as a preacher. On the other hand, preaching is a supernatural bestowal by the Holy Spirit of a speaking gift. You either have it or you don't. If, however, you have this gift, then you can develop it or squander it. You make that decision daily, depending on what you do with the opportunities God gives you.

Are you neglecting your gift of evangelism? Are you burying your gift in the ground? Are you taking great pains to improve your preaching? Would your friends say that you are a better preacher today than you were last year?

Examine yourself and your doctrine

And then Paul also exhorts Timothy to do two more very important things. He says that he is to pay close attention to himself and his teaching. What does this mean? First to pay close attention to himself is to examine his character. Is he a man of gospel holiness, or is he a phony and a hypocrite? Is he an impostor? Every believer is constantly to be vigilant about the deceitfulness of sin. Take bitterness as only one example. Paul exhorts the Ephesians, saying that all bitterness, wrath, anger, clamor, and slander must be removed from them, along with all malice, (Eph. 4:31). The Greek text of this verse makes clear that there is downward movement from bitterness, a seed sown in the heart which will grow, if not removed immediately. From bitterness comes wrath, which is an inward expression of anger. It is on the inside. The only possible outward manifestation of wrath is a rolling of the eyes or a sigh. Other people do not generally even know it is there. Anger, however, is an outward, quite evident and sometimes violent explosion of harsh, cutting, and cruel words.

Clamor goes further. Now the cat is out of the bag completely and the bitter, angry person's speech is dominated by verbal outbursts. The idea here is that these outbursts are quite common and regular occurrences. Slander is evident when the person no longer keeps the hostility to one or two or three people, but actually spreads the poison to many people every day. I have seen a woman whose husband greatly neglected her for many years take every opportunity she could to tell me of her husband's shortcomings. I am not saying that the husband was not guilty of neglect, because I think he was. Nonetheless, the woman has allowed her bitterness to fester, and now she slanders him.

And finally we come to malice. The Greek word used here was also used in the secular literature of the New Testament era to refer to a hailstorm which has cut down the wheat in the fields just a week before the scheduled harvest. The wheat lies in the field rotting. It is good for nothing. That's the picture of malice in this passage. Someone who allows a root of bitterness to spring up in his life will quickly become bitter. Then inward wrath and outward anger set in, followed by obvious clamor, slander, and malice. So it is very important that the evangelist keep short accounts with God and his heart. Are you bitter or angry? Do you "lose it" regularly. Are you slandering your boss, your wife, your friends, your business competitors?

Paul goes further, however, and exhorts Timothy to also pay close attention to his teaching, to his doctrine. This is vital. Most cult leaders started off being fairly orthodox in their theology, but went astray. Paul warns Timothy about these men (1Tim. 1:6,7). You must never be a "lone ranger." You need accountability from your pastor and elders. Continually ask yourself, "Does my preaching and teaching conform to the biblical norm?" Biblical confessions such as the *Westminster Confession of Faith* can be a guardrail against heretical or unorthodox teachings. Read it and also study the Scriptural footnotes. Become well versed in the texts of Scripture from which you are preaching. Be ruthless in your personal examination of the doctrinal content of your preaching. Guard your heart and mind against the encroachment of indwelling sin and heresy which is always crouching at the door of your soul.

A call to arms

Another passage which needs our attention is found in Paul's second epistle to Timothy in chapter four. The entire book is vital, but I am choosing presently to focus on verses 1-8:

I solemnly exhort you in the presence of God and of Christ Jesus, who is to judge the living and the dead, and by His appearing and His kingdom: preach the word; be ready in season and out of season; correct, rebuke, and exhort, with great patience and instruction. For the time will come when they will not tolerate sound doctrine; but wanting to have their ears tickled, they will accumulate for themselves teachers in accordance with their own desires, and they will turn their ears away from the truth and will turn aside to myths. But as for you, be sober in all things, endure hardship, do the work of an evangelist, fulfill your ministry. For I am already being poured out as a drink offering, and the time of my departure has come. I have fought the good fight, I have finished the course, I have kept the faith; In the future there is reserved for me the crown of righteousness, which the Lord, the righteous Judge, will award to me on that day; and not only to me, but also to all who have loved His appearing.

We choose to focus our attention here on the commands to Timothy. First, "Preach the word." The Greek word used here is *kerusso* which means to proclaim, to announce without equivocation. The idea is of one appointed by a king to take the king's message to his new subjects. The "town crier" gathers the people and gives verbatim the king's message. He does not alter it. He does not put his own spin on the message. He is not stressed if the people choose to ignore it. His only task is to be faithful. You, my friends, are to proclaim the word of God. You do not have the freedom or luxury to say what you want to say, to say what you think you should say. Preach the text of Scripture and call your hearers to obey the word coming from the King of Glory. To go further, you are commanded to correct, rebuke, and to exhort with the word of God you are proclaiming. If you see error in what your audience is saying, doing, or believing, then your task is to correct the error using the word of God. You are also to rebuke with the word of God. This is a very strong word that includes the idea of warning. Failure to heed the word of correction means unwanted and harmful consequences. And you are to exhort. This word means action. Do something. Just do it. Obey the word. Let's remember that Jesus is the conquering and exalted King, sitting at the right hand of His Father with all power. We are to call men, women, and children everywhere to submit to the King.

He then gives four more commands. Paul says, "Be sober in all things." Another way of putting this is to show self-restraint in all things. The flesh, world, and the devil are always tempting us, seeking to draw us away from simplicity and purity of devotion to Christ. We must constantly resist these temptations. How do you find the world, flesh, and devil tempting you? Paul puts it another way in 1 Timothy 4:7, "Discipline yourself for the purpose of godliness." Learn to curb your appetites for food, drink, or anything like books, movies, and videos which could weaken your faith and resolve to perfect holiness in the fear of God.

Paul also commands Timothy to endure hardship. He again says something similar earlier in his second epistle, "Suffer hardship with me as a good soldier of Christ Jesus" (2 Tim. 2:3). Paul goes on in chapter two to say he has suffered hardship even to imprisonment and that he willingly endured it so that those who are chosen of God may obtain the salvation which is in Christ Jesus and with it, eternal glory. He also says that all who desire to live godly in Christ Jesus will be persecuted (2 Tim. 3:12), not "may be persecuted," but "will be persecuted." And Jesus reminds us that when we are persecuted for the sake of righteousness that our persecutors are actually doing us a huge favor for our reward in heaven will be great (Mat. 5:11, 12). He also told us that if the world hates us then we should not be surprised because the world hates Him as well (John 15:18, 19).

And then Paul tells Timothy to do the work of an evangelist. It appears that Timothy was not an evangelist either in his gifting or in the office. Nonetheless, as a young pastor who was to teach others the same thing he had been learning from Paul (2 Tim. 2:2), he was regularly to reach out to the lost. If you are reading this book, then you more than likely are highly motivated to evangelize the lost, to publish the glad tidings of great joy to the lost world. However, even if you are highly motivated to evangelize, no doubt there are times when your flesh is weak and screams at you, "Not today." Maybe you have been receiving a great deal of opposition. Maybe your church is non-supportive. Maybe you are discouraged with a lack of financial support. Maybe those who have been regularly going to the streets with you moved away or have lost interest and you feel that you are isolated. Whenever these thoughts and feelings come upon you, discipline yourself to get back out there, remembering that the Lord Jesus is with you by the Spirit, that His word never returns empty, that it always accomplishes the purpose for which God sent it, and that you will reap in due time if you sow and do not faint.

And then the final word from Paul in this exhortation is to fulfill your ministry. Has God called you to preach the word? If the answer is "yes" then you must go. You are to go and do your best according to your skill, study, and experience so that you may preach the word of God and call people to repent and believe the gospel on the spot. You are responsible to go and do your best. God is responsible to bring the results He has foreordained. Are you exercising the gifts and calling of God on your life? How have you been doing of late? Have you grown lethargic, disinterested? Are you discouraged, fearful? Are you cold hearted, hard hearted, or have you lost your passion for souls? It happens to all of us. When all is said and done, we all are mere men. The best of men are men at best. But run back to the lover of your soul, the One who constantly is interceding for you at the right hand of the Father. Ask Him for grace. If you seek Him, then He will let you find Him if you seek for Him with all your heart.

Scripture saturation

There are many other passages we could examine in light of our
calling as evangelists, but let's consider one more. One of the
most important is Colossians 3:16, "Let the word of Christ
richly dwell within you, with all wisdom teaching and admon-
ishing one another with psalms and hymns and spiritual songs,
singing with thankfulness in your hearts to God." I wish to
focus only on one aspect of this verse. Let the word of God
dwell richly within you. I call this "Scripture saturation." You
must intentionally take in the word of God. How so? Consider
the words of King David, "Thy word I have treasured in my
heart, that I may not sin against Thee" (Psalm 119:11).

If we wish to be blameless (Psalm 119:1), if we hope to be
blessed (Psalm 119:2), if we desire to live righteously (Psalm
119:3), if we want a shame-free life (Psalm 119:6), if we long
for lives marked by a spirit of thanksgiving (Psalm 119:7), if
we want to be marked by purity (Psalm 119:9), and if we long
to prevent apostasy or wandering from the true faith (Psalm
119:10), then we must treasure God's word in our hearts. This
is the remedy to overcome sin in thought, word, and deed.
Scripture saturation must be a core value. To treasure something is to hold it in high regard. I treasure my wife, children,
daughters-in-law, and grandchildren. I treasure my health. I
treasure my close friends. I treasure my books. That is, I go to
great lengths to preserve and improve those things dear to me.
You, no doubt, do the same.

To treasure God's word in our hearts, in the very essence of
our being, is to be very careful to take it into our lives and to
act upon it (Mat. 7:24-27). In light of the multitudinous ways
our minds, eyes, ears, and consequently our hearts are bom-
barded with error, it is vital that we become soaked, saturated,
satiated with Scripture. You cannot get enough Bible. Jeremiah
says that he found and ate the words of God, that they became
the joy and delight of his heart (Jer. 15:16). Jesus said that we
live by the word of God (Mat. 4:4). The writer to the Hebrews

calls it a sharp and two-edged sword that pierces the division between soul and spirit and is able to judge the thoughts and intentions of the human heart (Heb. 4:12). David said that it was his meditation all day long (Psalm 119:97).

What, then, do I mean by Scripture saturation and how do we do it? Every Christian, and this includes every evangelist, ought to set aside some time every day, preferably in the morning (Psalm 5:3), to read God's word in a systematic fashion. There are many tools available to help you with this. However, the manner in which you read it is vital. Reading the Bible merely to get through the reading of the day, to check it off your "to do" list is no good. To read it merely for its literary value will not feed your soul either. And, reading it only with your mind short circuits its sanctifying power in your life. Instead, you are to read the Bible in "Three D," with your mind, heart, and will. You are to read your daily allotment of Scripture as though you are reading it for the first time. You are to read it existentially. Put yourself into the life situation of the text. When you read 1 Samuel 17, David's battle with Goliath, vividly see the story in your mind. Ask God to cause you to come alive to the text by the Spirit. And after you have read the passages for the day, ask yourself this question, "So what?" What does this mean practically for me this day? With the acrostic SPECK, you can ask more specifically—is there any *sin* to avoid, is there any *promise* to claim, is there any *example* to follow, is there any *command* to obey, and is there any new *knowledge* of God, myself, or the world that I learned today, and what difference can this make it my life? How will I obey today what I just read?

And since the word of God treasured in our hearts keeps us from sin and promotes righteous living, does it not stand to reason that we ought to be in the word several times per day? William Wilberforce, the great emancipator of the slaves, spent an hour in the morning, an hour at noon, and an hour at night soaking his mind, heart, and will in the word of God. He often recited all one hundred and seventy-six verses of Psalm 119 on his nightly walk home from the British Parliament. Perhaps you should find the time to read two chapters of the Bible in the morning, one at lunch time, and one in the evening.

Scripture memorization and sermons

But I suggest that true Scripture saturation is also aided by Scripture memorization. Early in my Christian life, while Bill Gothard was speaking to fifteen thousand people at a time, for a full week, I remember being amazed at the amount of Scripture he had committed to memory. I have sought to follow his example since that time. It is much harder today than it was in the beginning, but setting aside time each morning for daily memorization work and systematically reviewing chapters I have learned in the past has been a wonderful encouragement to me as an evangelist.

While you are driving to work, while you are exercising, or while you are working around the house, download sermons from great preachers and listen to them. Pray for your pastor that he may be gripped by God's word so that he may preach it to you in the power of the Spirit. Go to church each Lord's Day expecting to hear a word from God. And finally, spend a few minutes a day reading great Christian literature. There is so much wonderful material available to us today—from the Reformers of the 16th century to the Puritans of the 17th century, to the great revival preachers and theologians of the 18th century, to the godly men and women of the last two centuries. But read and listen with a distinct purpose— to have the word grip your mind, heart, and will so that you may become more and more like Jesus. Obey what you know. Because the Bible is the infallible, inerrant, and inspired word of God, it is your lifeline. Soak your soul in it. In so doing, you will go deeply with God, and this will bear fruit in your evangelistic ministry.

Advice for Evangelists— Prayer and Going

As we look now at some advice for evangelists, it is imperative that we consider prayer. We know that we all say we believe in prayer, but the evangelist must be convinced that, without the visitation of the Holy Spirit upon evangelistic efforts, nothing will happen. There is no transforming power of the gospel in a ministry plan or a dynamic pastor or preacher. There are plenty of churches growing numerically which are way off-base theologically and practically. We must have the power of the Spirit to lead us to people of peace and to convict them of their sin and need for Christ as the only Savior of sinners.

The foundation of prayer

What, then, must we do? We must gain an intolerable burden. Until we have it, nothing else we do will avail much at all. We can go on with our planning, programs, personalities, building, and budgets, but we will continue to lose ground in our culture.

Without the intolerable burden, we are kidding ourselves. This is absolutely essential. So what is the intolerable burden? It is an intense agony, grief, and alarm over the *status quo* in our personal lives, in the church, and in the world. The Scriptures are replete with men and women who exhibit the intolerable burden. Take Daniel, a contemporary of Jeremiah and Ezekiel, for example. By the ninth chapter of his prophecy, he tells us that he is reading the prophet Jeremiah, who prophesies a return from the Babylonian captivity in seventy years (Dan. 9:2, Jer. 25:11-12, 29:10). This revelation serves at least two purposes in his life. First, it is like a lifeline to a drowning man. There he is, in dismay, discouragement, and devastation. He has witnessed firsthand the devastation of Judah by Nebuchadnezzar and his hoards. Daniel knows that the judgment is just, but he nonetheless, in exile himself, is deeply burdened. So, he begins to seek God by prayer and supplications (earnest and fervent prayer), with fasting, sackcloth, and ashes, confessing his own sins and the sins of the people. He says, "We have sinned, committed iniquity, turning aside from Your commandments and ordinances." He goes on to say, "Righteousness belongs to You, O Lord, but to us open shame." He goes still further, beseeching the Lord, "Let now Your anger and Your wrath turn away from Your city Jerusalem, Your holy mountain." He asks the Lord to hear his prayer, to shine His face on the people, to incline His ear, to see the desolation of the city. He appeals not to any merits in himself or the people, for they have none. Rather, he appeals to the Lord's great compassion (Dan. 9:4-19). His intense grief over the *status quo* drives Daniel to contrition, confession, supplication, and intercession.

If we are to understand and engage in revival prayer, then we must have a strong and solid foundation. That foundation begins first with the intolerable burden. Do you have it? Do you have an intense agony, grief, and alarm over the *status quo* in your own life, the church, and the world? What do I mean by the *status quo* in your own life? We could go to many places in

Scripture for the answer to this question, but perhaps the best place to look is Jesus' letters to the seven churches of Asia Minor in Revelation 2-3. Only two of these churches receive a clean bill of health from Jesus (the church at Smyrna and the church at Philadelphia). The other five are commended in various ways but also condemned as well. Take, for example, the church at Ephesus. Paul the Apostle came there at the end of his second missionary journey and then returned on his third journey, spending three years there. The church was planted around AD 53. We know from Acts 19 that God was working mightily in Ephesus. Demons were being cast out. Those involved in witchcraft were burning their books and fetishes, departing once and for all from them, determining to follow Jesus at all costs. And in the city where the great temple of Diana was located, the worship of this false goddess was suffering greatly because so many had turned from their idols to serve the true and living God. Paul wrote his letter to the church at Ephesus while he was in a Roman prison around AD 62, putting down glorious doctrine in the first three chapters, following in the last three with a series of commands for those living in the church of Jesus. But by the time we get to the book of Revelation, written around AD 66, Jesus tells the church at Ephesus that, though they have perseverance and cannot tolerate evil men, and though they put to the test those who call themselves apostles but are not, and though they have endured for the sake of Jesus' name, He is against them because they have left their first love (Rev. 2:1-4).

Think about it—in less than fifteen years, this once great and mighty church is accused of leaving its first love! What are the characteristics of this dynamic love they had for Jesus? They were known for their great faith in the Lord Jesus and their sincere love for the brethren (Eph. 1:15). Paul called them God's workmanship, created in Christ Jesus for good works which God prepared beforehand for them to walk in them (Eph. 2:10). He calls them fellow citizens with the saints, being of the household of God (Eph. 2:19). He says that they are God's beloved children (Eph. 5:1), and that, though they were formerly darkness, they now have become light in the Lord (Eph. 5:8-9). They were zealous, hungry for Christ, committed to the work of His kingdom; but that is all gone by AD 66, thirteen years after the church was established.

My friends, we must have an intolerable burden, an intense agony, grief, and alarm over the *status quo* in our own lives. Have you left your first love? Do you remember how it was when Christ Jesus first revealed Himself to you? If you were like me, you could not get enough of God's word. You loved good, Biblical preaching. You were there every time the door to the church was opened. You attended Bible studies. You were hungry to learn all you could, and you had a simple faith. If God said it, that settled it, and you obeyed it! And though you may have been rough and unpolished in your evangelistic efforts, you nonetheless could not stop speaking about Jesus. You talked to anyone who would listen about Him. Jesus was on your lips at all times. You seemed always to get Him into every conversation. You were moved by singing the great hymns of the faith. Your sin grieved you. You lived with a constant state of awe and amazement, that your sins were forgiven, that you were declared innocent by God, given the very righteousness of Jesus. You knew that you were an heir of God and a fellow heir with Jesus. You believed that God was working everything in your life for good because you loved Him and were called by Him.

But perhaps now you are ambivalent about preaching and going to church. You can take it or leave it. You seldom spend much more than a perfunctory time reading the word and uttering a brief prayer as you go out the door to work, preferring on your commute to listen to sports talk radio rather than gospel preaching. It used to be that you were at church Sunday morning, Sunday night, Wednesday night, and one other night during the week for Bible study or evangelistic visitation.

It used to be that foul words never crossed your lips but now secretly, and perhaps sometimes very openly, your speech is tainted with cursing, lewd comments, and sexual innuendo. It may be that the thought of marital infidelity no longer repulses you, that sexual fantasies constantly plague your mind and heart. It may be that you have lowered your standards on television programming, tolerating programs that you at one time would have considered abhorrent. You get the picture, don't you? Have you left your first love? If so, then repent and do the deeds which you did at first. Ask God once again to give you a hunger for His word, both in preaching and in your own personal study of it. Ask Him to make you repulsed by your sin and to give you the gift of repentance, that you no longer would grieve the Holy Spirit. Ask Him to give you a love and burden for the lost.

Intolerable burden for the church

But if we are to seek God earnestly in revival prayer, if we are again to see a great and mighty movement of the Spirit, then we must also gain an intolerable burden for the church. We must become deeply grieved with the *status quo* in the church of our day. Of course, there are wonderful exceptions, but surely you will agree with me that the church in the western world is in big trouble. The materialism, the worldliness, the licentiousness, the division, and the strife that results in church splits is everywhere. We now have evangelical pastors and leaders who doubt the historicity of Adam and Eve, who are not so sure that homosexuality sends people to hell, who question the inerrancy of Scripture. And again, with some wonderful exceptions, much of the preaching today is paltry, insipid, and lacking convicting, converting, and sanctifying power. Many preachers seem content to give information about the Bible, believing that their job merely is to disseminate information, failing to understand what Calvin, Knox, Edwards, Whitefield, Spurgeon, and Lloyd-Jones knew so well—that true Biblical preaching is logic of fire, that while there must be light, there must also be heat, that a preacher is to afflict the comfortable and comfort the afflicted, that he must take people to Mt. Sinai before he can adequately take them to Mt. Calvary. In other words, the preacher must constantly preach the terrors of the law, not only to convict the lost of their sin to drive them to Christ, but also to preach the law to believers, driving them again to Christ for repentance and growth in grace. And he must preach the law to the world, warning everyone from the President, the Supreme Court, Congress, and state and local legislators down to private citizens that they are not a law unto themselves, that they are accountable to the Great Judge who will judge them according to their deeds. The preacher is to be a prophet to the nations, to the universities, to Wall Street, and to Main Street. He is to be a comforter to those believers wounded in conscience. He is to use the word like a hammer to shatter the pride, unbelief, and rebellion of the smug, self-righteous, and comfortable. The church is to move away from her idol of comfort and ease and venture out into the world of pain and suffering, into the inner cities where little boys and girls do not have a father at home.

If your church is not marked by earnestness in prayer, powerful gospel preaching, lots of conversions, a mighty sense of the felt presence of God in your worship services, by growth in personal holiness in individuals and families, by selfless giving of time and money for kingdom expansion, by freedom and joy in everyone telling everyone they can about Jesus, by seeing the wickedness of the community dissipate, by seeing lots of men and women go into full-time Christian service, and by seeing the church become a major object to be reckoned with by the enemies of Christ—then your church needs revival. Your church needs the anointing of the Spirit. You ought to gain, therefore, an intolerable burden for your church, an intense grief and agony over the *status quo*.

Intolerable burden for the world

And while this burden is necessary for us and for the church, this intolerable burden needs also to grip us concerning our world. We could say so much here. You know the statistics. Our inner cities are in turmoil. The family everywhere is breaking down. Militant atheism is on the rise. We are losing our young people in droves, especially as they go off to college and university, unable to stand against the unbelief of Marxist college professors who poison their minds. Internet pornography is rendering millions of men intellectual zombies, enslaving them to their lusts where they prefer auto-stimulation to intercourse with their wives, robbing them of the focus they need to perform their jobs well, threatening to destroy their marriages, children, and careers. Young men are increasingly effeminate, preferring to stay at home well into their late twenties, unwilling to go out and get a productive job, unwilling to commit to marriage and rearing children. Increasingly, men stand on the job sidelines and the women are only too willing to take the jobs from them. We are not disparaging women at all. We don't blame them. The jobs are there for the taking, but men acquiesce, buying in unconsciously to the same old problem men have had since the fall into sin. Adam abdicated his responsibility, saying to God, "The woman, whom You gave to be with me, she gave me from the tree, and I ate" (Gen. 3:12), and men have been doing it ever since. "Why work, why take on responsibility, when I can get my wife to do it?"

And then there is the truth that all people who are not born-again are under the wrath of God and on their way to hell, a horrible place where the fire is never quenched and the worm never dies. It is beyond our comprehension or imagination how dreadful and awful hell is. Yet, that is not the end for the damned unbeliever. Upon Christ's return, all unbelievers will be brought before the judgment seat of Christ and give account of their deeds, whether good or bad. Their thoughts, words, and actions will all be judged, and they will hear the most awful words imaginable, "Depart from Me you workers of iniquity into the everlasting fire which has been prepared for the devil and his angels" (Mat. 25:41). This is where mobilization and going comes into play. When the evangelist senses this intolerable burden for the world, he won't stop at prayer. He will go to the world with the gospel.

Evangelists must go

Evangelists, gifted and called by God, sent out as missionary bands, can be of tremendous usefulness to the local church. Here are two very simple and practical ways for your church to go to the lost in your own town. The first way is to encourage your church members to make an *oikos* list and work their list. The Greek word *oikos* means *household,* and it appears over one hundred times in the Bible. A household is the web of relationships each person has. Their *oikos* would be their immediate family members, extended family members, neighbors, old friends from high school or college, work or business associates, and many others. For example, I have around one hundred and fifty names on my *oikos* list. Then, you can encourage your people to pray over their list each day or a few days each week. They should pray for the Holy Spirit to be working in the hearts of their friends and family members, bringing conviction of their sin, or perhaps a sense of emptiness in their lives. As your people are praying, encourage them to ask the Lord to direct them to their *oikos* members whom they should try to contact. They can call or visit people on their list and let them know they have been praying for them and would like to know of anything specifically for which they can pray. You will be surprised at how open and often how moved people are to know that others are willing to pray for them.

From there we can briefly tell our testimony of what we were like before becoming followers of Jesus, how this came about, and what changes Christ has made in our lives since that time. It is important we emphasize the work of Christ when giving our testimony. We can then ask, "Do you have a similar story?" If they say, "Yes," then you can say, "That's great. Would you mind telling me your story? I would love to hear it." If they say "No," then you can say, "Okay, would you like to know how God can work in your life?" If they say that they would like that, then you can briefly share the gospel with them. Just think what could happen in your church if every member made an *oikos* list and faithfully and prayerfully worked his or her list!

A second way to reach out with the good news of Jesus Christ is to go to four types of people in your community—*PIPS*. This comes directly from the words of the prophet Isaiah (Isa.61:1-2) from which Jesus reads in His first sermon in a synagogue in His hometown.

> *The Spirit of the Lord is on Me,*
> *because he has anointed Me*
> *to proclaim good news to the poor.*
> *He has sent Me to proclaim freedom for the prisoners*
> *and recovery of sight for the blind,*
> *to set the oppressed free,*
> *to proclaim the year of the Lord's favor.* (Luke 4:18, 19)

The first *P* stands for *poor*. In all our evangelistic work, especially door-to-door evangelism in many cities around the U.S. and Africa, we have found that poor people are generally much more receptive to speak to you about their need for Jesus. Oftentimes, there seems to be a built-in humility in them which is most often lacking in well educated, affluent people. In fact, Jesus said that it is easier for a camel to go through the eye of a needle than it is for a rich man to inherit the kingdom of heaven (Mat. 19:24). We are not saying that you should refrain from reaching out to people who have lots of money or a nice big house. We are only saying that you will generally find poor people much more open, and this is where you should spend most of your time, especially if you have already exhausted all the prospects on your *oikos* list.

Secondly, you should look for international students or immigrants who have recently moved to the United States. These represent the *I* in our acrostic. Most international students have never been in the home of an American. If you befriend students at your nearby university who are from other countries and invite them to your home, then they almost always will accept your offer. You can have a few of them come at once and share your custom of Christmas or other holidays and then ask them about their customs. From there, you can easily move into the gospel. And if they come to faith in Christ and then move back to their countries of origin, then you have been used by God to expand His gospel to other nations, as they will surely take their new faith back to their own people.

Immigrants are also usually very open to the gospel, and they typically stay in groups with people like them from the same country. At first, it may be difficult to break into the group, but if you have an inroad with one person, then you can say that you would like to meet many other of their friends. You can have them all to your house for a cookout and share the gospel. And since this group will have their own *oikos* if you reach one or two of them, then you very well may be able to reach most, if not all their web of relationships.

Thirdly, you should seriously consider reaching out to prisoners from the local, state, or federal prison. This is the second *P* in our acrostic. Evangelists can regularly go to the prisons and hold Bible studies where men or women can find out more of what God says in His word about how they can gain peace, purpose, and power in their lives. Oftentimes, prisoners have been humbled by their circumstances. They are pretty clear on the sin issue. They know that they have rebelled against God and society. That's why they are where they are. I remember one time preaching in a prison and I was in a holding cell where new prisoners were being processed, having only come there in the last day or two. You could see the fear on the faces of most of the men. Such people are generally very receptive to the good news of Jesus Christ. You can also find ways of ministering to prisoners upon their release from prison. They often need fellowship and encouragement.

And fourthly, you should be strategic in going to people who are sick. This represents the *S* in *PIPS*. In fact, in one of the countries where I work, the top entrance into gospel conversations with the locals is to ask if they are sick, and if so, can we pray for them. In this particular country just about everyone is sick. So we ask, "If God could do a miracle today in your life, what would it be?" Almost in every case they respond, "To heal me of this disease." Then we pray for them on the spot, asking God to bring healing. You can do the same with sick people in your neighborhood, and when you pray for them, expect God to heal them. This can be a very powerful means of drawing people to faith in Christ. When such people are healed, they see the power of God practically displayed. You will note that Jesus first came preaching the kingdom of God, but He also came healing people of disease and casting out demons (Mat. 4:23-25). So, our work is not merely preaching or evangelizing, nor is it only deeds of mercy. It is *both/and*.

The evangelist must be a person of prayer, but he also must be a person who goes. We see this demonstrated in the early chapters of Acts. Jesus commands the disciples to wait and pray before they go out. After receiving the Holy Spirit at Pentecost, they are ready to go, but not before then. To go to the world with the gospel is the most impossible task a person can attempt. We must have God move if anything is to be done. The evangelist must have the intolerable burden of prayer before he goes out to preach the gospel to all the nations.

The Evangelist's Character—A Puritan Case Study

First and foremost, you must seek God for the development of holiness in your personal life and in your wife and children. Nothing reflects more negatively on an evangelist than ungodly character. If an evangelist has good character, then churches will be more willing to work with him. The Greek philosopher Aristotle famously said that every orator must have three ingredients in his oratory—*logos, pathos,* and *ethos. Logos* refers to the content of his message. Is he speaking truth? Is his argument consistent? *Pathos* refers to the passion with which he communicates his message. Is he believable? Does he feel what he is proclaiming to others? *Ethos* refers to the ethical character of the speaker. Is he a man of morality? Does he practice what he preaches?

We have known men who were very solid on logos and pathos. They are theologically sound in what they preach. They speak with passion. They have an excellent delivery of their sermons. However, some of them are lacking in ethos. Their behavior, their values, their speech, their relationship with their wives in how they treat them in an unruly or dominating manner, and the waywardness of some of their children cast doubt on the veracity of their ministries.

In order to illustrate the vital necessity of character in a preacher of the gospel, consider a brief biographical sketch on the Puritan preacher, Cotton Mather. We can learn much from him. There were many, many good things to glean from his life but there were also some troubling things which ought to serve as a sober warning for all of us.

Cotton Mather was one of the greatest scholars our country has produced, a man of unusual intellect and Christian piety. In his day, he was loved by many and reviled by some. In our day, he evokes emotions of awe and respect, as well as anger and disdain. Cotton Mather has inspired the faith of many and undermined the faith of others. Indeed, he was a Puritan enigma. Cotton Mather was born in 1663, thirty-three years after John Winthrop and other Puritans sailed from England and established the Massachusetts Bay Colony in Boston. The Pilgrims were separatists who wanted nothing to do with the Church of England. They had settled the Plymouth Colony in 1620, led by William Bradford. Now a generation after their arrival, the Puritans of Boston were thriving. Cotton Mather was named after his two illustrious grandfathers (John Cotton and Richard Matherwas, born to Increase and Maria Mather). Both of Mather's grandfathers were educated at Cambridge, the hotbed of Puritanism in the day, and both migrated to America after persecution at the hands of William Laud and the Anglican leaders in England.

Cotton Mather was exceedingly precocious, reading and writing before he was six years old, becoming fluent in Latin by age eight, and taking extensive notes on his father's sermons in Latin by the time he was nine years old. He was trained in the Classical tradition, reading the works of Cato, Tully, Ovid, and Virgil in the original languages before he was eleven. He also became fluent in the Greek New Testament and Hebrew Old Testament. He is the youngest student to ever enter Harvard, having done so at the age of eleven, beating his father by six months or so. Due to his age and small stature, life was not easy for Cotton at Harvard. Increase removed him from Harvard for a season due to the severe hazing he was experiencing. With his young age came the zeal by which he rebuked older students for their lack of holiness and spiritual deportment. This no doubt did not help his relationship with other students.

Cotton Mather came from a long line of preachers, and with his grasp of Latin, Greek, and Hebrew, he was clearly equipped to become a powerful Puritan preacher. However, he had one humbling problem. He stuttered. No one is certain of the cause of stuttering, but some have suggested that it comes to children prior to puberty due to parents placing unrealistic expectations on their children. We don't know if this was true with Increase, but it is perfectly clear that the Mather men expected great things from Cotton. So, being one who stuttered was the most humbling of circumstances for him, as it would be for any preacher. Elijah Corbet, an aging educator living near Harvard, gave Mather advice he practiced for the rest of his life. He was to sing the Psalms. That's because hardly anyone stutters when they sing. Second, he was to speak very slowly and deliberately, as though he was drawling his words, almost as though singing. Apparently, the stuttering never left Mather, but he did learn how to overcome it by the means prescribed by Corbet.

Mather made a practice of writing nearly every day of his life. He had beautiful handwriting and made over five thousand pages of sermon notes from his father and other Puritan preachers of his day. He kept a daily journal, much of which has survived to this day, and he constantly wrote books, the two most extensive and well known of which are *Magnalia Christi Americana,* a history on the mighty works of Christ in America up until his day, and the *Biblia Americana,* a sort of running commentary on the Bible and Biblical themes which he worked on for over fifty years. In all, Mather published over three hundred and fifty books. He was awarded a Doctor of Divinity from the University of Glasgow for his *Magnalia*. Furthermore, he had a lifelong interest in science, being made a member of the *Royal Academy* in Scotland. He regularly corresponded with scientists in England and Scotland and lived at a time when the scientific method was coming to be accepted, and the old Aristotelian explanation of science was rapidly passing from the scene.

Cotton Mather gave evidence of regenerating grace as a young teen. The Puritans, while practicing infant baptism and rearing their children to believe on Christ and walk with Him all their days, also believed that one must have a conversion experience and give evidence of an inward change before one could be admitted to the Lord's Supper. Many Puritans preached *preparationism,* that is, that one must seek God for a long period, giving themselves to daily repentance in hopes that the peace of Christ would flood their souls. Cotton experienced this during his time at Harvard and, though he briefly considered medicine as a profession, there was very little doubt that he would follow his father and grandfathers into the pastoral ministry. Upon his graduation from Harvard at fifteen, Cotton preached his first sermon at sixteen. He tutored students for a few years and then was offered the pastoral position at the Congregational Church in New Haven, Connecticut when he was nineteen. He refused it, believing that he ought to stay in Boston. The people of the North Church, where his father was the pastor, overwhelmingly voted to call him to serve with his father as a pastor in the church. He waited a few years, believing that he was too young and inexperienced for such a role, but eventually agreed, serving this church until his death in 1728. Cotton threw himself into every aspect of the pastoral ministry at the North Church, preaching regularly, visiting the sick and dying, performing weddings (fifty-two of them in 1709 alone) and funerals, and catechizing the children. The Puritan form of ministry in his day had a lecture on Thursday, which was like a sermon, usually an hour and fifteen minutes in length, and two sermons on Sundays, each an hour and a half long. Increase and Cotton Mather divided these duties, and when Increase traveled to England for three years, Cotton took over the full pastoral duties and performed them admirably.

Cotton Mather apparently had a temper and was given to outbursts of anger. He sought to curb this and other sinful tendencies by doing good to all men. He wrote a book entitled *Bonifacius* in 1712 where he put forth his ideas. Benjamin Franklin read this as a young man, saying that it utterly changed his life, moving him to be a doer of good all his days. Cotton battled a desire to be well known as a preacher and writer on the one hand with a desire to walk humbly with God on the other.

He obviously was a powerful preacher of God's word, telling younger preachers to prepare for preaching by going directly to the pulpit from their knees in prayer. They were to begin slowly, in a low tone, expounding the text, giving the theological implications, answering objections which may arise in the text, and then move to application. At this juncture they were to rise in animation and voice. On one occasion Cotton had to apologize to his congregation after praying for two hours in his pastoral prayer. He then preached for an hour and a half.

There can be no question that Cotton Mather was a man deeply devoted to Christ. His long hours in his study reading, writing, and composing sermons; his tireless pastoral visitation, fearlessly going into the homes of those ravaged by smallpox and measles; his courageous stand against the spiritual declension in his beloved New England which he believed would bring God's judgment on the town of Boston; and his regular practice of fast days where he devoted himself to whole days of prayer and fasting for the salvation of his people all point to a man of unusual devotion to Christ.

Like all men, however, there were a few areas of great weakness in his theology and practice. For one thing, at least two long periods of his life were given to what he believed was communion with angels. The first occurrence was just after the Salem Witch Trials of the early 1690's and the second was during the last ten years of his life when he had the three-fold trouble of his marriage, his child Creasy, and impending financial ruin. He believed in the existence of angels and that God had given them to His children for their support and comfort. So far so good, as all Evangelical Christian theologians believe this, but he took it further, saying that he actually spoke with angels who gave him messages of assurance from time to time. Another strange practice, which he learned from his father, was what he called *presagious impressions*. He would often sense very strongly a certain event which was soon to happen. For example, he received a very strong impression that his second wife would become ill and die. He also believed that God would visit Boston with a terrible sickness, and this later played out in the measles epidemic which killed his wife, servant, and three of his children. When he later married his third wife, he was convinced that she would marry him, though she at first resisted his overtures. Mather was not the first nor the last to believe strongly in God-given impressions, but the danger is to believe that these are absolutely infallible, that they will certainly take place. Mather did not always receive such impressions with a degree of skepticism or reserve.

Also, Cotton Mather was a major player in the infamous Salem Witch Trials. Consider this excerpt on Mather from Nathaniel Hawthorne's *Alice Doane's Appeal*:

> "In the rear of the procession rode a figure on horseback, so darkly conspicuous, so sternly triumphant, that my hearers mistook him for the visible presence of the fiend himself, but it was only his good friend, Cotton Mather, proud of his well won dignity, as the representative of all the hateful features of his time, the one bloodthirsty man, in whom were concentrated those vices of spirit and errors of opinion that sufficed to madden the whole surrounding multitude."

This is not to suggest that Nathaniel Hawthorne did not have impious biases against Mather, which was likely the case. But it is not exactly wrong, either. Mather believed that witches and Satanic activity were real, that proven witches ought to be executed, but that extreme caution must be used in following through with execution. He and others believed that the most important evidence to convict a witch was a credible confession, where the accused actually confessed to being a witch. A questionable method was to use what they called spectral evidence, when people would testify against an accused witch, saying that they had seen the accused engage in bizarre and wicked behavior. On more than one occasion, people said that they saw so-called witches flying about on brooms, wearing cone hats, and mixing a devil's brew which they gave to unsuspecting victims. One man, for example, said that a witch appeared to him at night, waking him from a deep sleep by sitting on his stomach. Mather warned against too much use of spectral evidence, but to no avail. By the end of 1693, nineteen women and one man had been found guilty and executed as witches. Many others were imprisoned. Children were testifying against their parents, brothers against their sisters, neighbors against their neighbors. A panic had overtaken the town. In the end, several ministers came to the forefront, calling for the suspension of the trials. Eventually this took place and the frenzy ended.

How, you may ask, could this happen when the Puritans, especially Cotton Mather, were so committed to ruling their lives and churches by the Bible? Perhaps one explanation is that the new science of Isaac Newton and others was rapidly eroding belief in the unseen world. Some of the Puritans surmised that a rejection of belief in witches would cause people eventually to deny the existence of God, which would spell the demise of the supernatural Christian faith. It is inaccurate to say that the Puritans alone were reckless in the witch trials, for many others, including Roman Catholics, were given to the same thing. The Puritans seemed to attempt to deal with each case systematically, using caution. However, Cotton Mather and the Puritans, while believing in the supernatural world of Satan and demonic activity, failed to evaluate these things totally in the light of Scripture. Their behavior in general, and Cotton Mather's in particular, was inexcusable and reprehensible, and perhaps has done more than anything to impugn the great benefits of the Puritan theology and life.

Cotton Mather's life was one great hardship and trial after another. Shortly after his twenty-third birthday in 1686, Cotton began seeing Abigail Phillips, a young woman who was sixteen years of age, the daughter of Colonel John Phillips, a justice of the peace and a man prominent in military affairs in Boston. Cotton sought her hand in marriage as diligently as he did his pursuit of holiness in Christ. He spent one day every week fasting and praying, asking that God would give him favor with her. After a brief courtship of three months, they were married at the North Church and they immediately moved into a house his father, Increase, had used after a fire had destroyed his original house. Cotton was uncertain of Abigail's spiritual state and prayed daily for her salvation, instructing her in God's word, urging her to pursue Christ. Eventually, she came to an assurance of her salvation and became a communing member of the North Church.

In May, 1702, after sixteen years of marriage, Abigail miscarried at four months of her pregnancy, and Cotton sensed a dark cloud hanging over his family. It may be that Abigail suffered from breast cancer and Cotton watched his dear wife sink deeper and deeper into sickness, culminating in her death in November of that year. She briefly revived in August after a vision of God where she was told to place a fresh patch of wool from a living sheep on her painful breast. The pain subsided for a time, and they both had hopes of her full recovery, but it was not to be. She was buried beside their five children who had died before her. Shortly after Abigail's death, their eight year old daughter Nibby nearly died from a smallpox epidemic, and during this time Cotton's house was a hospital as smallpox ravaged their family and servants.

A year or so later, Cotton married a second time. He married Elizabeth Hubbard Clark, who was also several years younger than him. He brought his four surviving children into the marriage and they all readily accepted Elizabeth as their new mother. Their union produced another five children. Though Cotton was incredibly busy with his ministry of preaching and writing, he found time daily to rear his children in the nurture and admonition of the Lord. He often spoke against the common practice of his day of verbally maligning children. He said that this was an abomination and that children should be instructed straightforwardly and lovingly, speaking kindly and gently to them. He said that as soon as they are old enough to understand their need of Christ, a parent ought to pray for his children in their presence, weeping over them for their salvation.

Another outbreak of measles visited Boston in 1713 and ravaged the city, including his own family. Elizabeth died shortly after giving birth to twins. A few days later, both of the twins died too, and finally another daughter died. Later that year, his mother died at the age of seventy-two. About this time, Mather entered a note in his journal saying that, of his fifteen children, nine were dead. In all these trials, Mather accepted them as the will of God, rejoicing in the hope he had for his dear wives and children being in the presence of Jesus.

Several months after Elizabeth's death, a young woman, aged twenty-three, began pursuing Cotton, saying that she wished to marry him because he would be good for her soul, hopefully drawing her to the Savior. Cotton resisted her advances for a season, but eventually was flattered by her interest in a man who was fifty years old. They began seeing each other and the people of Boston were talking about his inappropriate relationship with her. Cotton finally realized that this could be harmful to his ministry and sought to put her off. She continued to pursue him, even recruiting her mother to convince Cotton that he ought to marry her. There does not seem to be any illicit sexual activity between them, but surely his ministry was in jeopardy. After breaking off his relationship with her, she threatened to tell the community the details of their courtship. Cotton was fearful that she would spread untruths and tarnish his ministry and the name of the Lord Jesus Christ. He fasted several times, asking the Lord to cause her to drop her threats to harm him and his ministry. A short time later, Cotton received a letter from her saying that she would not bother him again. He saw this as a great and merciful visitation from God on his behalf.

He then turned his attention to Lydia Lee George, a young woman whose husband had died a month earlier. Lydia Lee's father was a very wealthy man and Lydia Lee's first husband had been well to do as well. He first visited her with one of his young children. He persisted in pursuing her, and Lydia Lee at first rejected his advances, telling him in no uncertain terms that she was not interested in him. Cotton continued his pursuit, going through mutual friends. Eventually, Lydia Lee softened and the two were married, placing a pre-nuptial agreement on their marriage. Lydia Lee had been a member of the Brattle Street Church, which was viewed by many as a rather liberal church. She was worldly, materialistic, manipulative, and perhaps even psychopathic. While Cotton saw the spiritual beauty of his first two wives, physical attraction and the comforts of Lydia Lee's wealth seem to be the driving force behind his courtship of her. A year or so after their marriage, Cotton began entering into his journal in Latin a number of troubling reports of her "prodigious paroxysms." While both Abigail and Elizabeth were models of Puritan piety and self-control, Lydia Lee was given to outbursts of anger which often lasted for days. Cotton was deeply grieved at her behavior, wondering what he had done to provoke it. She maligned him as well as his children. On one occasion, she left him for several months, bringing great embarrassment and heartache, not to mention the negative talk of church members and others in the city of Boston. There would be long periods of peace, but these always were followed by more outbursts. She even threatened to return to the Brattle Street Church. These persisted to the end of Mather's life, some ten years after their marriage. A year after his marriage to Lydia Lee, Catherine became the tenth of his children to die. Her death apparently was from the lingering effects of the measles epidemic of 1713.

Then, there was the financial hardship which Cotton incurred from his marriage to Lydia Lee. Lydia's first husband, at his death, had an import business which had many accounts. Cotton thought it wise to serve his new wife by becoming what today we may call the executor of her first husband's estate. Cotton thought that this would be a rather simple affair. He would collect the money due the business and pay whatever outstanding bills came. He was certain that the assets were more than the liabilities. He was wrong. Cotton faced one lawsuit after another for the last ten years of his life, a time when many men are able to enjoy a relative amount of peace and prosperity. Lydia Lee was unwilling to part with any of her own money to satisfy her first husband's debts, looking to Cotton to cover them with his meager pastor's salary. This was humiliating for Cotton, since he had long told his parishioners to refrain from debt, believing such brought great shame to Christ. Now he was a man in great debt and the whole town new it.

Then, there was the case of his wayward son, Increase, nicknamed Creasy, who held such promise as a scholar and pastor. Creasy had many of the same intellectual gifts as his father and grandfather and was moving toward Harvard and the gospel ministry when he began to lose interest in his studies and the pursuit of God. Finally, he dropped out of college and became a sailor, sailing the seas and living the notorious lifestyle of sailors. Cotton tried numerous times to bring his son back to Christ, having him copy his sermon notes, discussing them regularly, and praying with and for his son. Nothing seemed to work. Finally, after several years of praying and fasting for his son, Cotton received word that his son had died at sea. Later he was told this was a mistake and he rejoiced, only to discover that this too was inaccurate information. Creasy had died, and Cotton lived with the fear and sorrow that his son had died without Christ, rejecting the very Savior he had earlier said he would serve.

Cotton suffered many trials throughout his entire life, but the last ten years were the most severe. Though filled with sorrow, he continued to seek Christ humbly, preaching regularly, serving his congregation, and writing his numerous books. As an evangelist working with local churches, what can you learn from Cotton Mather's life? When studying the lives of great men and women, we see their many strengths are outweighed to some degree by their foibles. The best of men are men at best.

Without question, Cotton Mather's major trials in life were the big three that we mentioned earlier—women, money, and children. It does not seem as though Cotton was guilty of any sexual sin, but he allowed his flesh to cloud his thinking in marrying Lydia Lee. He was flattered by her, and he also thought that she had a great deal of money, and this was apparently a motivating factor in his pursuit of her. In the end, his marriage to her was a disaster. Evangelists must be careful in these areas, always vigilant. And the waywardness of Creasy cannot, of course, be placed primarily on Cotton. At the end of the day, our grown children are responsible for their own walks with Christ. However, we can at least wonder if there was something lacking in Cotton's relationship with his son.

I choose now, however, to focus on four of his great strengths—things we ought to emulate ourselves. The context is in regard to evangelists and their relationships with churches. First is what I call his *sanctified scholarship*. Mather was a man of prodigious intellect, and this was proven by his large library, fluency in Hebrew, Latin, and Greek, his authorship of three hundred and fifty books, and his keen interest in medicine. In a day when science was encroaching on absolute truth as it is found in holy Scripture, when so many were jettisoning revealed religion, that which is found in the Bible, Mather tried diligently to subject his mind to Scripture as his only infallible rule of faith and practice. He did not always succeed, as seen in his major failure in the Salem Witch Trials, but this generally characterized his life. Those with great intellectual gifts, who are believers in the Lord Jesus, do well to follow Mather's example. He sought to evaluate all areas of life through the lens of Scripture and he never tired, even to the end of his life, to keep up his fluency in Latin, Greek, and Hebrew. He was a pastor first, but with this came a deep love for theology which pervaded his life. He spent time every day reading theology, studying and meditating on Scripture, and writing. All students of God's word, including evangelists, would do well to follow his practice of reading challenging books on theology and the Christian life. Writing also makes an exact person, so whether you hope to be published or not, you should still write.

Second is *the blessing of his godly heritage*. Both his grandfathers, numerous uncles, and one of his own sons were all in the gospel ministry in New England. More importantly, they were men who lived above reproach, not falling to the numerous temptations which face ministers and evangelists. He sought to pray with his children and instruct them in the Christian life. He took seriously their baptisms into the covenant of grace and labored with them for their own salvation in Christ. Here is a vision all men ought to seek. Perhaps you did not have the benefit of a godly upbringing, but you now know the vital necessity of one, and you would do well to purpose now that you and your household will serve the Lord. If we are to see the values in our nation return to Biblical faith, then it must start at the home, and more specifically it must begin with the heads of our households. Men must put aside the false notion that their job primarily is to make money, that upon arrival at home in the evening they are free to sit in front of a television and leave the Biblical instruction and character development of his children to his wife. Your most valued possession is your wife and children, and you must consciously, willfully, and consistently establish your authority as their leader in your home.

Third is Mather's *pursuit of experiential holiness*. The tendency of too many Biblical scholars is to settle for scholarship devoid of heartfelt passion for Christ. Mather would have none of this. His life was marked by heart and mind fully devoted to the Lord Jesus and the progress of the gospel. He was very conscious of his propensity for rebellion and outright evil against God. He generally was vigilant to not allow himself to be placed in compromising circumstances. He practiced the Puritan principle of mortification, putting to death the deeds of the body by the Spirit. He was careful to not feed the evil desires in his heart. He spent long periods daily in prayer and Bible study. He fasted regularly, and he interpreted the events of his life in light of God's dealings with him. He was always searching for a message in whatever trial came his way, and as we have seen, they were many. He kept short accounts with God and regularly confessed his sin to Him, and then to those against whom he had sinned. He had a tender conscience which, when violated, gave him no peace until he had settled the issue with God. His deep love was the Lord Jesus Christ, and he sought regularly to develop his relationship with Christ. Mather sought to see God in all of life's circumstances. When tragedy or trial struck, he regularly asked himself, "Have I sinned against God? Is He contending with me for some reason?" You would do well to follow Mather's example.

And fourth is his *perseverance under trial*. My friends, as an evangelist you will certainly have your share of trials. The devil is always working against the servants of God to tempt them and to discourage them. Clearly people of Mather's day saw death on a regular basis, and the death of their own children was too often a sad reality. Even though infant mortality was pervasive, no doubt the pain and sorrow of losing a loved one was always very real to the Puritans. This was clearly the case with Mather, but while there was sorrow and grief, it is clear that such grief was mitigated by his close walk with the Lord. There is no indication in his books or journals of a paralyzing grief or anger when God's frowning providence fell upon him and his family. Could this be because Mather was so heavenly minded? His trials drove Him to Christ, who alone brought him true comfort. He lived as though heaven was as real to him as the Boston in which he lived. He believed in the resurrection of the dead, that due to Christ's death and resurrection, all who have believed in Him have the promise of eternal life, that at the moment of death they would open their eyes in the glorious presence of the lover of their souls. This made more palatable the bitter pill of death which he so often tasted. I urge you to ground your faith firmly on the bigness of the Puritan God and His Christ. This faith will stand you well when the deep waters of trial, tragedy, and death overflow you.

Cotton Mather was a Puritan enigma. He was a great pastor, preacher, evangelist, and theologian. He was a wonderful father and husband. He was a scholar and writer who made marvelous contributions to the work of Christ in our world. He was, however, a major player in the Salem Witch Trials. He could fall into pride, made manifest in the self-promotion of many of his books. He could hold grudges, and speak unkindly of those who disagreed with him, but he was a man who always came back to the cross of the Lord Jesus Christ, knowing that his only boast was in the cross of Christ, to which the world had been crucified to him, and he to the world.

Biblical character—what is it?

What is the Biblical character you should ask God to develop in your life so that you can be the most effective evangelist possible? There are many, but let's focus briefly on these.

First is humility. Humility can be defined as a modest view of one's own importance. A humble person knows who God is and His glorious attributes and power, but also knows who he is and never confuses the two. "God resists the proud but gives grace to the humble" (James 4:6). "Whoever humbles himself like a child is the greatest in the kingdom of heaven" (Mat. 18:4). "For everyone who exalts himself will be humbled and he who humbles himself will be exalted" (Luke 14:11).

Second is servanthood. Servanthood means acting in the role of a servant. A servant is a person who performs duties for others. In the Biblical sense he is a slave with no rights. "Paul a bond servant of Christ Jesus, called as an apostle" (Rom. 1:1). "Jesus emptied Himself, taking the form of a bondservant" (Phil. 2:7).

Third is faithfulness. Faithfulness comes from a place of trust and loyalty. Hebrews 11:1 says, "Now faith is a confidence in what we hope for and assurance about what we do not see." As a Christian, it is important to be faithful to God. If we are faithless, He remains faithful for He cannot deny Himself (2 Tim. 2:13). "Faithful is He who calls you and He will also bring it to pass" (1 Thes. 5:24).

Fourth is availability, which means making your own schedule and priorities secondary to the wishes of those whom you are serving. "Then I heard the voice of the Lord saying, 'Whom shall I send? And who will go for us? And I said, 'Here am I. Send me!'" (Isa. 6:8). "And Jesus said to them, 'Follow Me, and I will have you become fishers of men.' Immediately they left their nets and followed Him" (Mark 1:17-18). "If you fully obey the Lord your God and carefully follow all His commands I give you today, the Lord your God will set you high above all the nations on earth. All these blessings will come on you and accompany you if you obey the Lord your God. You will be blessed in the city and blessed in the country" (Deut. 28:1-3)

Fifth is teachableness. You are teachable if you are aware of the limitations of your own knowledge and abilities, if you admit limitation, inability, and ignorance to others who can teach and help you, and if you are aware of the limitations of your own knowledge and abilities. "Likewise, you who are younger, be subject to the elders. Clothe yourselves, all of you, with humility toward one another, for God opposes the proud but gives grace to the humble" (1 Pet. 5:5). "Whoever loves discipline loves knowledge, but he who hates reproof is stupid" (Prov. 12:1). "Poverty and disgrace come to him who ignores instruction, but whoever heeds reproof is honored" (Prov. 13:18). "And we impart this in words not taught by human wisdom but taught by the Spirit, interpreting spiritual truths to those who are spiritual. The natural man does not accept the things of the Spirit of God, for they are foolishness to him, and he is not able to understand them because they are spiritually discerned" (1 Cor. 2:13, 14). "Give instruction to a wise man, and he will be still wiser; teach a righteous man, and he will increase in learning" (Prov. 9:9).

Sixth is patience. This character quality implies suffering, enduring, or waiting as a determination of the will and not simply from necessity. It is to wait for God, to endure uncomplainingly the various forms of sufferings, wrongs, and evils that we meet with, and to bear patiently with injustices which we cannot remedy and provocations we cannot remove. It is important we realize patience originates from God. "For whatever was written in earlier times was written for our instruction, so that through perseverance and the encouragement of the Scriptures we might have hope. Now may the God who gives perseverance and encouragement grant you to be of the same mind with one another, according to Christ Jesus, so that with one purpose and one voice you may glorify the God and Father of our Lord Jesus Christ" (Rom. 15:4-6). Patience is part of the fruit of the Spirit, "But the fruit of the Spirit is love, joy, peace, patience, kindness, goodness, faithfulness, gentleness, self-control; against such things there is no law" (Gal. 5:22). We can also go further and say that patience is a product of self-control and is a part of Godliness, "and in your knowledge, self-control, and in your self-control, perseverance, and in your perseverance, godliness" (2 Pet. 1:6). Patience was demonstrated by Christ,

"He was oppressed and He was afflicted, yet He did not open His mouth, like a lamb that is led to slaughter, and like a sheep that is silent before its shearers, so He did not open His mouth" (Isa. 53:7). Patience is a character quality which helps us grow during trials, "And not only this, but we also celebrate in our tribulations, knowing that tribulation brings about perseverance; and perseverance, proven character; and proven character, hope; and hope does not disappoint because the love of God has been poured out within our hearts through the Holy Spirit who was given to us" (Rom. 5:3-5). "Consider it all joy, my brethren, when you encounter various trials, knowing that the testing of your faith produces endurance. And let endurance have its perfect result, so that you may be perfect and complete, lacking in nothing" (James 1:3-4). Patience allows us to be strengthened and blessed by God, "I would have despaired unless I had believed that I would see the goodness of the Lord in the land of the living. Wait for the Lord; Be strong and let your heart take courage; Yes, wait for the Lord" (Psalm 27:13, 14). "Yet those who wait for the Lord will gain new strength; They will mount up with wings like eagles. They will run and not get tired. They will walk and not become weary" (Isa. 40:31). Patience is also pleasing to God. "The end of a matter is better than its beginning; Patience of spirit is better than haughtiness of spirit" (Eccl. 7:8). "But in everything commending ourselves as servants of God, in much endurance, in afflictions, in hardships, in distresses" (2 Cor. 6:4).

Seventh is submissiveness. This is vital to an evangelist who seeks to serve his own local church. Submissiveness means giving up your own rights and freedom so that you are directed by another person. We see this played out in the marriage relationship. "Wives are to submit to their own husbands" (Eph. 5:22-24), and all of us are to submit to one another (Eph. 5:21). We also are to submit to governing authorities. "Every person is to be in subjection to the governing authorities. For there is no authority except from God, and those which exist are established by God. Therefore whoever resists authority has opposed the ordinance of God; and they who have opposed will receive condemnation upon themselves. For rulers are not a cause of fear for good behavior, but for evil. Do you want to have no fear of authority? Do what is good and you will have praise from the same" (Rom. 13:1-3).

Eighth is prudence, which is a very important quality for anyone engaged in ministry, but especially so of the evangelist. He is on the street regularly. We run into all kinds of difficult situations like young women exposing their breasts while we are preaching or seeing very wicked behavior at Gay Pride Parades. Prudence is careful, wise discernment. It is the avoidance of rash behavior or speech. It is the good management of talents and resources and the showing of tact and wisdom in relationships with other people. "The simple believe anything, but the prudent give thought to their steps" (Prov. 14:15). "A fool's anger is known at once, but a prudent man conceals dishonor" (Prov. 12:16). A prudent man also possesses foresight and exercises caution. "The prudent sees the evil and hides himself, but the naive go on, and are punished for it" (Prov. 22:3). "When you sit down to dine with a ruler, consider carefully what is before you, and put a knife to your throat if you are a man of great appetite. Do not desire his delicacies, for it is deceptive food" (Prov. 23:1-3). A prudent person also makes wise use of knowledge and is very careful in his speech. "A prudent person conceals knowledge, but the heart of fools proclaims foolishness" (Prov. 12:23). "Let your speech always be with grace, as though seasoned with salt, so that you will know how you should respond to each person" (Col. 4:6). "He who guards his mouth and his tongue, guards his soul from troubles" (Prov. 21:23).

Lastly, vigilance. We can define vigilance as being watchful, circumspect, careful, and attentive to discover and avoid danger or to provide for safety. Paul tells the Ephesian believers "to be careful how you walk, not as unwise men but as

wise, making the most of your time because the days are evil"
(Eph. 5:15, 16). He instructs Timothy, his child in the faith,
to be sober in all things (2 Tim. 4:5). Special Operations men
in our military are vigilant when they are on a mission. As they
enter a compound to free an American hostage, they are looking
for trouble in every direction. They are well-prepared. They
know exactly what they are to do, and they are well prepared for
every possibility. Peter tells us to be on the alert, to be sober in
spirit. In other words, we are to be vigilant. Why? Because our
enemy the devil is like a roaring lion, roaming about to devour
whomever he may (1 Pet. 5:8). The devil hates you, your family,
and especially your evangelistic work. While you are not to fear
the devil, you most certainly ought to know very well they he
can tempt you and destroy your family and ministry, causing
you to bring disrepute to Christ's church.

Working with Churches

One of the most important aspects of an evangelist's ministry will be his relationship with other churches. Evangelists should constantly be working with other churches, difficult as it may be at times. Evangelists should not be laboring in a vacuum. We will address this important issue with three major points—character, vision, and ministry.

You can be a great encouragement to a local church by sharing your vision of what God can do through the church. I remember several years ago being asked by the pastor of a local church to speak to their elders. The church was a downtown church in decline. The preaching was sound, the people were loving, but the church had almost no local evangelistic outreach. To be sure, the church supported world missionaries, but as far as reaching their own community and city, nothing. I sought to give the elders some vision of what God could do. I told them that many years before in downtown Philadelphia, James Boice became the Pastor of Tenth Presbyterian Church. Through a long, faithful, and productive pulpit ministry, all manner of ministries developed out of the church. These included a ministry to homosexuals, a crisis pregnancy center, a ministry to the many college students in their city, and a Classical Christian School for urban children. I told the church elders that they were sitting on a gold mine, that they were very near a major medical center and university, and several Section 8 housing projects were nearby. They would need to begin with earnest prayer, asking God to raise up evangelists who would be willing to go to the surrounding community with the gospel. They prayed and, over the next several years, God has sent that church numerous evangelists who are training people and sending them out to the university, medical center, and surrounding housing developments.

Because most pastors are not gifted evangelists, they do not have an eye for what God can do in their communities. They often have a "deer in the headlight" look. They tend to be paralyzed and unwilling or unable to evangelize. You can help give them vision. How so? Many formerly Evangelical churches or denominations are moving away from the simplicity of evangelizing and discipling the nations. The moment a pastor or church leadership believes their job is to redeem the culture or to bring *shalom* to the community is the moment they begin to accommodate with the world. Cultural accommodation always leads to some form of modernism, which can be defined as a "self-conscious adaptation of faith to the modern world; the idea that, to minister effectively, we must take on ingredients of the modern world." This means that the church needs to show that they are woke, hip, cool, and relevant, which means that they must jettison Biblical doctrines and Biblical worship.

So, how can you give them a vision to get back to the basics of the Bible? First, you must have godly character. Pursue a holiness of life. Perfect holiness in the fear of God. As you have been part of your church for some time, pray about God opening doors of ministry for you in your church. Do not push this. Don't rush it. Allow God to go before you. Spend time with your pastor and the elders of the church. Sooner or later, they will ask you what you do in work or your ministry. You can then tell them and suggest that they "come and see" what you do, whether it is open air preaching at a university or abortion clinic, or whether it is one-on-one street evangelism or door-to-door ministry. Most believers have a pretty lousy connotation of these forms of evangelism, and you can allay their fears by asking them to come along with you and watch.

From there you can give statistics about the perceived number of true believers in your city and ask how the churches can reach them. Here's an example of something I wrote to recruit pastors, evangelists, and church planters to a training program I will be hosting.

> I have known all but one or two of you for many years now and I am writing to each of you because I know you have a keen desire to reach people with the gospel of our Lord Jesus Christ. Some of you are pastors, others are evangelists, and still others are interested in planting churches. Some of you are now in Vanguard Presbytery. Others of you are in the PCA or OPC, or in independent churches, but I think all of you sense that the way of planting churches in the U.S. is not working very well.

> I believe a lot of us are frustrated at the way things are going in the church. We spend enormous amounts of money and rarely see conversions. If we add up the entire cost of "doing church" in the U.S. and divide that by the number of adult baptisms in a single year, the cost per baptism is $1.5 million. And the number of Evangelicals in our nation is not keeping up with our population growth. Now, only 7% are born-again—that's around 26 million people. Furthermore, the big donors to churches and ministries are baby boomers, and they are dying off.

> The simple fact is that younger people are not giving to evangelism, missions, or church planting as their

parents were. Within ten years, many church leaders are projecting that money for these causes will shrink significantly. Our method of "doing church" is unsustainable. Furthermore, it is not Biblical. Most of our growth is transfer growth, what I call "shuffling the deck." I believe we have departed from the clear, simple, and easily taught methodology we find in the gospels and the book of Acts. I have been studying this issue for several years now and I am coming to the realization that we must evangelize, disciple, and plant churches God's way. I am speaking here of multiplication and not merely addition. We don't need vast sums of money to plant churches. We all pray for and want revival, but have we asked ourselves exactly how God may bring it? There must be massive numbers of conversions, but how are they going to come?

In my search to learn more about how to plant churches, I have come across Bill Laky. Bill is a church planter and pastor in Cape May, New Jersey. Bill is Reformed in his theology and ecclesiology, which gives me a great level of comfort when we speak about multiplying disciples and churches. Bill is willing to teach us, free of charge, how to plant churches and multiply disciples from a Biblical perspective. Bill has a congregation of about 150 people and has seen over 60 adults converted and baptized in the last year or so. That's pretty amazing for a Reformed pastor, especially one in New Jersey.

I am inviting you to join Bill and me for three months, every Wednesday night, beginning January 13 from 8 p.m. to 10 p.m. Eastern time, 7 p.m. to 9 p.m. Central time through a Zoom link. We will be limiting the Zoom conference to eight or ten people because we want to make sure we have good interaction. If we have more than this number, then one of Bill's elders who is also an experienced trainer will take the other group.

I especially hope any of you connected with Vanguard Presbytery will take us up on this offer. This is not a "silver bullet." This is not some hip, cool program. This is merely looking at the Bible and seeing what Jesus and the apostles did and seeking to imitate them. This is very simple, but I believe it cuts across the grain for most of us, including myself. All we have ever known is some form of an "attraction" model, build it and they will come. My vision is to see God multiply evangelists, church planters, and disciple makers who in turn multiply churches throughout this country.

I have had a very good response to this invitation. This is an example of what you might do to cast a vision for your local church for evangelistic ministry which sees many conversions and multiplies disciples. We must have many more evangelists. So why not say to the leaders of your church, "In light of our present distress as a nation and church, it seems to me that we must have evangelists. The attraction model (if we build it, they will come) is not working in our nation. It is far too expensive and cuts off laypeople from intentional and powerful multiplication in ministry. The church as it presently operates in our country is grown by addition. We add a church here, a church there, perhaps over many years and spend inordinate amounts of money to do so. There is a better way. There is a Biblical way, and it is a way of multiplication.

We are seeking to motivate you, to give you a vision and practical skills on how you can be a most effective evangelist, using your gift for the expansion of Christ's church. One of the most practical ways you can do so is through helping a church plant other churches. How then should we plant churches? How can you assist in this most worthy endeavor?

Planting churches

Consider first of all how churches are traditionally planted in the United States. Typically an Elder Board or Session (the elders of a local church), usually under the able leadership of their pastor who has a vision and passion for church planting, approves the decision to plant another church. Sometimes Presbyteries (the regional group of churches in a Presbyterian denomination), or a consortium of independent churches (such as in the Southern Baptist Convention or Acts 29), or the Bishop of a district in the United Methodist Church (which has an Episcopal form of church government) make this decision. So, how do they decide where to plant a church, how do they plan to fund the work, and how do they plan to grow the church plant to viability?

Typically, they survey a community. Usually they are looking for a new, fast growing part of town which may not yet have too many churches. They also tend to choose areas which are affluent, often believing that if they can reach this affluent community then there will be money available for further church plants as well as developing "missional" opportunities at home and abroad. Then they (what we call the "mother church") look for "seed" families from a congregation. These folks usually have been traveling some distance to church and would like to have one closer to their homes. Then the Church, Session, or Presbytery calls a church planter. Usually they will put up some money to pay the church planter's salary and ministry expenses, but the church planter is typically expected to raise a good portion of the budget. Depending on where the target area for the new church is and the cost of living, the church planting budget will be quite expensive. During that time, the church plant is expected to grow to the point where the church is self-supporting. The church planter must also be a "gatherer," usually a dynamic personality, an engaging speaker, a people person. And from where do the new people come? They are usually Christians who are moving into the new, fast-growing community, or perhaps they are believers who have become dissatisfied with their old church for various reasons. Sometimes, especially in the Reformed world, they are former Arminians who have found R.C. Sproul and other Reformed preachers and writers and want to find a Reformed church. While there is much talk of evangelism, these church plants rarely reach lost people in their communities.

The traditional model of church planting is also big on demographics. The traditional church planter is expected to "exegete his community," to know what the people like and dislike, how they view the world, whether they watch *Fox News* or *MSNBC*. He is to decide on his target audience. He must decide if he is going after Boomers, Gen Xers, Millennials, or Gen Zers. He is to become part of the community. He is to join various clubs so that he can meet people. He is to join a local workout facility, or better yet, join a *CrossFit* group. It is assumed that, by building relationships with these people, he can eventually, perhaps six months to a year down the road, earn the right to be heard and begin exploring the possibility of faith with these people who now trust him. He typically spends a great deal of time reading books on church growth strategy and the corporate leadership model as well as attending church planting conferences so that he can understand the sociology of his community and what techniques work best.

Here's our simple question—is this the model we find in the gospels and Acts? Is this the approach our Lord Jesus or the Apostle Paul used? Not at all. We challenge you to read though the gospels and Acts and see how they did church planting.

Simply put, they were dependent upon the Holy Spirit. Jesus did not begin His ministry until the Spirit came upon Him at His baptism. The apostles were told to stay in Jerusalem until they were clothed with power from on high. At Pentecost, the Spirit came, and with Him, the power for gospel ministry. You will note that neither Jesus nor Paul had any guaranteed salary. Jesus was poor. Paul was a tentmaker. The Philippians

helped Paul financially, but they were the only congregation
to do so (Phil. 4:15-16). Neither Jesus nor Paul wasted time
"exegeting" the culture. They were on mission. They did not
have time to hang out with people for a year or two, waiting to
earn the right to be heard. They knew heaven and hell were at
stake. They understood that they were to work as long as it is
day, for the night was coming when no man could work. Jesus
went to more than one hundred and fifty towns and villages in
Galilee, which were no more than a one or two days walk from
Capernaum. It probably took him a full year to do it. Paul produced church planting movements in four Roman provinces in
about ten years. It appears that, after his first release from prison,
having not been able to plant churches for a few years, he traveled to Crete, Illyricum (modern day Croatia), and Nicopolis
in Italy (near the ancient city of Actium, made famous by Mark
Anthony and Cleopatra about one hundred years earlier) and
planted churches in all these places. He may have also made it
to Spain (the end of the world in their view) before his second
imprisonment and subsequent martyrdom in Rome.

And what did Jesus and Paul do? They modeled multiplication. At best traditional church planting, by the very nature of
how it is done, can only be by addition. One church now, and
perhaps in five or six years, another church can be planted. Paul
was all about multiplying churches. He spent three years in
Ephesus, yet we know of at least eight more churches planted in
that region. Paul was first an evangelist, as was Jesus. Paul went
first to the Jews and reasoned with them from the Scriptures
that Jesus is the Christ. After they rejected him, which always
happened, Paul turned to the Gentiles and proclaimed Jesus to
them. Paul was the consummate evangelist and street preacher.
He used open air preaching to get the gospel out to as many
people as possible, but he also went house-to-house (Acts
20:20), as did the other apostles (Acts 5:42). He also spent time
in the agora in Athens, the market, the ruins of which are still
present today, just down the pathway from Mars Hill, the site

of his Areopagus address. Paul also picked up on Jesus' teaching to His disciples (Mat. 10:12, Mark 5:19, 20, and Luke 10:6, 7) about *oikos*, the Greek word for household, which is used 106 times in the Bible. Paul reached Lydia's household and the Jailer's household in Philippi (Acts 16), and herein lies the secret of their success. Lydia and the Jailer told their own *oikos,* their crews, their entourages, their families about Jesus and they responded positively. And these new believers, who understood the amazing deliverance from sin, Satan, death, and hell, were zealous to proclaim Jesus to their neighbors and family. They could not stop speaking what they had seen and heard. They also did not waste time with those who were not open. They were looking for people of peace. They had no specific target group. They preached to whomever was open. They followed the Spirit's leading. Paul wanted to go to Asia Minor, Mysia, and Bithynia, but the Spirit did not permit him. He ended up in Macedonia. They were reaching lost people, mainly pagans from horribly licentious lifestyles. Paul and his crew willingly accepted the abuse and scorn of the religious leaders and the elites, the movers and shakers of their world. They rejoiced to be called spectacles to the world, fools, idiots, unlearned, the scum of the world, and the dregs of all things.

Here's our question—shall we be traditional or Biblical in church planting? Some may say, "What Paul and Jesus did is not necessarily prescriptive." I object and say, "Sure it is. The Scriptures are our only authority. We would do well to follow Jesus and Paul in how they got things done." There is so much more which could be said.

This is the way we are seeking to plant churches in Vanguard Presbytery. This is the way churches should be planted in your own denomination or church. You are an evangelist. The church needs you desperately. Evangelism is the spearpoint of any church ministry. It is not the only thing which is to be done, but after prayer, it is certainly the first thing to do. This work will clearly fail if we do not have the Holy Spirit empowering us and leading us. I have every reason to believe, however, that He is raising up men to engage in evangelistic work with the expressed purpose of planting churches. This is perhaps the greatest gift you can give to your own local church. We should expect mighty things from God. These are exciting times in which to live.

The emphasis must be on multiplication of disciples, to become disciple makers. I dare say that very few evangelists or pastors intentionally or deliberately multiply disciples. Yes, we may disciple a few people here and there, but perhaps a better word for what we tend to do is mentoring. We mentor, bring along, or encourage young men toward pastoral or evangelistic ministry, but seldom do we find men who are discipling people to three or four generations. This is how we can make a powerful and significant impact on our world.

Think of it this way, our country is so far gone and the church is so compromised that we need thousands of evangelists regularly on the streets of our nation. Evangelists are to be the conscience of the nation and church. They are to warn people, as the Old Testament prophets did, of impending judgment for all who do not seek refuge in Jesus Christ. We preach the message of judgment at the abortion clinic, in front of restaurants and night clubs, at the universities, at ball games, and at state and federal courts, or wherever we can find the opportunity and wherever people gather. We preach Christ crucified, to the Jews a stumbling block and to the Greeks foolishness, but to all who are called, Christ the wisdom of God and the power of God. Open air preaching is a broadcast of the gospel. It is like the "carpet bombing" employed by the Allied forces in World War II against Germany. It was done from thousands of feet above the earth. It works to "soften up" the enemy.

Paul reminded the Ephesian elders of his house-to-house ministry (Acts 20:20). Luke reports that every day, in the temple and from house-to-house, they kept right on teaching and preaching Jesus as the Christ (Acts 5:42). Jesus told the seventy to go to every city, door-to-door, and look for people of peace (Luke 10:1ff). So, our advice is that you grasp this material and look for opportunities to cast this vision of faithful, fruitful multiplication of evangelists and disciple makers in your local church.

When the church is not excited

What should you do if your church is not excited about your ministry, if they choose not to support you? What should you do if they discourage you from evangelism or if they want to soften the tone or methodology of your ministry? Unfortunately, we have spoken with many men who find themselves in this predicament. And what are the objections which you tend to face?

"You are not ordained. Therefore, you do not have the authority to street preach or witness." My friends, we need to move past our western traditions and get back to the Bible. What do we find there? We find that everyone is evangelizing (Acts 8:4, Col.1:5-8, 1 Thes. 1:7-8). We find Peter expecting everyone who has been called from darkness to light to proclaim Christ's excellencies (1 Pet. 2:9-10). Do we not see in the Scriptures what the reformers of the 16th century called the "priesthood of all believers?" The so-called clergy/laity distinction is not found in the Bible. Everyone is to teach the truth, everyone is to evangelize, and everyone is to show mercy to the fatherless and widow. We will never reach our communities if the unbiblical view of church membership prevails. And what is that? People are expected to join a church, come on Sunday, listen to the sermon, learn from the pastor or other gifted teachers, give their money to pay for the multi-staff, ordained leadership, and perhaps serve in the nursery, teach children's Sunday School, or bake cookies for folks who may venture into the Reformation Day party. The attraction model of ministry is alive and well, but it is also killing the church. We will never reach the lost in our communities until the leadership unleashes their members and gives them the freedom to engage in whatever ministry God may direct them to do.

"Street preaching and intentional evangelism does not work. It is too controversial. People react negatively against it." We hear this all the time. First of all, according to the Scriptures, any time the gospel is preached it "works." Isaiah tells us that the preached word never returns empty; it always accomplishes the purpose for which it is sent (Isa. 55:11). Sometimes, people are humbled and return to the Lord for grace and forgiveness. Sometimes, the preached word is the first or second link in the chain which ultimately draws the person to sincere faith in Christ. Sometimes your hearers hate the word, and their judgment becomes greater. Paul said that the preached word is a savor of life unto life or death unto death, and who is sufficient for these things? We have often been asked, "In your street preaching, how many people have you lead to Christ?" We always say, "All of them. I am leading people who listen to the glory and excellencies of Christ's person and work, but only God can apply that word in a saving fashion to them. Salvation is a sovereign work of a sovereign God. Our job is to be faithful, to sow the gospel seed, to water the seed which may have been cast earlier. It is God's business to bring it to fruition."

Others say that street preaching and cold-call or intentional evangelism is too controversial, that many people react negatively to it. First of all, we will be the first to admit that some street preachers are beyond the pale. Some of them by their tone and content are unnecessarily alienating people. Some are disrespectful of their audience and get into arguments with them or call then names. This is reprehensible. I remember one of the first times I preached in the open air I was with a guy who did this regularly in his town on Saturday afternoons. He used a very loud amplification system which blasted the folks sitting in a park who, in a leisurely fashion, were eating picnic lunches with their families and friends. Many of the people were irritated by the preaching. Sure, they perhaps were irritated by the content of true gospel preaching, which we were doing, but I suspect their greater objection was to the fact that we were intruding on their right to enjoy a nice afternoon in the park without interruption. I would have probably resented to some degree a preacher doing that if I was having a picnic with my family.

So clearly, we must be respectful of other people and try to be as Biblical as we can be in our preaching. Having said this, however, we must also acknowledge that open air preaching, even when it is done respectfully and biblically is still controversial for many. Should this then cause us to refrain from preaching? Not at all. Again, what do we find in the ministries of Jesus and His apostles? They were regularly engaged in open air preaching, as were the Old Testament prophets. They were beaten, stoned, and left for dead on many occasions. The very fact that open air preaching is controversial is no reason to not engage in it.

Furthermore, some object by saying a lot of people react negatively to it. Assuming that we are being Biblical in the content of our preaching and that we are respectful, we should not be at all surprised by the fact that people react negatively to it. Remember that the natural man considers Biblical preaching as foolishness. He hates God. He does not receive the message because he is dead in his sins. So, of course, people react negatively. Paul certainly faced this everywhere he went. He outlines for us the suffering he faced (2 Cor. 11:23-29). So, you are in good company when you suffer for preaching Christ in the open air.

Still others will say that door-to-door evangelism is too time consuming and does not give much "bang for the buck." But we see Paul engaging in it (Acts 20:20) and we find Luke telling us that the early church was going house-to-house (Acts 5:42). Our model is the Lord Jesus, who in Luke 10 tells the seventy to go in twos to the various towns in the area and look for people of peace, for those who are open to the good news. So, when we go house-to-house, I always tell people to not worry about those who do not answer the door, who are rude, or who show no interest. Instead, you are looking for the one or two who are open, who perhaps are presently encountering some serious problem. It very well may be that God brought you to their door for a time such as that. If every church would devote two hours per week to door-to-door evangelism in their neighborhoods and find only one person of peace each week, then those churches would have fifty or sixty "prospects" with whom they could teach an evangelistic Bible study, meet some specific mercy ministry need, or simply pray for the people on the spot and ask God to do a miracle in their lives. Nothing is wasted in the economy of God. There is no substitute for "boots on the ground." It is hard work, but quite necessary if we are serious about ministering to the people in our communities.

Seeking resolution

Sadly, the evangelist might face ostracism from his local church for his evangelistic activity. We are not ignorant of the challenges of maintaining a good relationship between the local church and evangelists, even in churches that are healthy. Historically there seems to be a tendency for the local church to shun or criticize these preachers, oftentimes coming from the leadership. Likewise, evangelists have tended to shun and criticize the local church, especially the leadership. Where do such tendencies come from? How can they be resolved? There exist at least four principal reasons for the conflict. These are not exhaustive, though they are common. These reasons do not justify either the evangelist or the local church in criticizing the other. But perhaps, if we put a finger on the sources of conflict, it will help avoid such dissension.

First, many local churches, including Reformed churches, are cold and ossified in matters of evangelism. Their members are comfortable in their non-evangelism and sharing the gospel to the lost, as a church would be a strange novelty. They are stuck in the general routines of work, family, church, and sleep. They might diligently attend prayer meetings and Bible studies. But the thought of serving the Lord outside church walls, especially sharing the gospel with strangers, seems odious. Whenever someone is doing evangelism and challenging others to do the same, congregants in general may feel convicted for not doing it. They may also feel threatened. To be challenged to do something other than the normal routine may appear offensive, and usually the one active in evangelism and challenging others to join will be the one to blame. But church members will not always say this aloud. To vocalize such an opinion would be to betray their dislike for evangelism, which would be the same as betraying their dislike for the Savior, since evangelism is a direct command from Him. In such a case, they will either avoid the preacher or criticize him on some other front. The reaction will be passive-aggressive. They may try to stop his call to evangelize by attacking his character or preaching style or something else. They may say that the evangelist will bring a bad reputation to the church, which gives them an excuse to refrain from sharing the gospel with strangers. This kind of response can come from the laymen as well as from pastors and elders.

Second, there is the problem of discomfort caused by evangelism, especially when it is bold and unpragmatic. Many in the local church, if pressed, would never approve of it. Most have been immersed in a church culture that is seeker-friendly, tolerant of sin, and terrified of offending anyone. Even born-again members of biblical churches have been influenced by the watered-down Evangelicalism of our day. Many have been taught that forming friendships and building houses is the best way to evangelize, and they view open air preaching as too brash or cutting. This is a typical reaction of a church culture steeped in unbiblical methods of evangelism. Some in the church may come out a few times with the preacher, excited to join the work, but typically, when exposed to the tension of preaching on the streets, these people decide that it is not for them. Moreover, some of them will decide it is not for the lost either. When exposed to the depravity of man and the response unbelievers show toward the preaching of the cross, they will not only never participate again but will express concern about any Christian going into the public square and preaching God's truth boldly. Many in the local church believe not only that open air preaching is the wrong way to evangelize, but that it is harmful. They will point to the lack of fruit or the impropriety of raising the voice for Christ. The local church is often embarrassed by these preachers.

Third, the church leadership often shows little support for evangelism. If the evangelist does not have the backing of his church leaders, he will soon be pressed into a corner and ostracized by the whole body. The leadership's response toward the preacher will be reflected by the congregation. Pastors and elders do not have to openly denounce the work of evangelism to show their disapproval of it. If they aim to be biblical, they will know that they could not openly denounce it. To do so would be to denounce the Bible. But leaders can show disapproval of public evangelism by their actions or lack thereof. If they do not encourage the body to support the preacher, join him on the streets, or at the very least publicly pray for him, then neither will the church. The leadership also may feel intimidated by his zeal and courage. This is not to puff up the preacher—he should know that any courage he has comes from the Lord, not himself—but the leadership may fear that the congregation will see them as less zealous because they do not join the street work, which can create friction between the church and the preacher.

Fourth, the church leadership may regard preaching on the streets as "easy," or a kind of lesser ministry compared to preaching from the pulpit, feeding the flock, and making home visits. The evangelist should show patience to such reactions, while at the same time encouraging the critics of this sort to join him one day on the streets. Anyone who has participated in this ministry, whether evangelizing or coming alongside one who does, is usually astonished by how taxing it is. The evangelist is frequently besieged by attacks from unbelievers, "believers," police officers, heat or cold or wind or rain, thirst and hunger, and the fatigue of standing on your feet for long hours, not to mention the demands on the emotions and vocal cords.

There is also the common, unhealthy scenario of the evangelist doing nearly all of the church's evangelism. The church merely relegates to the evangelist the duty of gospel proclamation to the lost and assumes it has done its evangelism duties by doing so. Ideally there will be a healthy interaction between the evangelist's evangelism and that done by the rest of the congregation. Churches can support the evangelist by having a team of people praying for him, by joining him to hand out gospel tracts and engaging in evangelistic conversation, or even by giving monetarily to cover living expenses or evangelistic resources like tracts or voice amplifiers. Likewise, the evangelist could help the church by coming alongside brothers and sisters who want to do more evangelism but are not as seasoned.

What should you do if and when you hear from the pastor or church leaders, "Your type of evangelism is not welcome here. This is just not how we do it."? Simply put, assuming it is not a character issue or some other grievance that is the problem, leave and find a church that will at the very least pray for you and encourage you in their ministry. Don't waste your time with a church which has no interest in evangelistic outreach. Even if they do not like door-to-door work or street preaching, they should at least acknowledge the Biblical origin of such ministry from a historical perspective. However, if they will not do that, then move on to another church. Don't be resentful, but rather grieve for that church. Don't be divisive or disrespectful. Work with the church to see if they come around, but if not, prayerfully consider a change. The church may have a large staff, a multi-million dollar budget, and a beautiful church building with several thousand members. But a church which is not supportive of gifted and called evangelists is dying.

The Evangelist's Pitfalls

Having laid the foundation for some practical advice to evangelists, we now need to consider several of the pitfalls all evangelists face on a regular basis. The devil hates you, your wife, your children, and your ministry. He wants to bring you down, to make shipwreck of your faith, and to ruin your life in every way possible. Never underestimate the evil one. This is perhaps the most important chapter of the entire book, because if the evangelist stumbles here, nothing else in the book will matter very much.

Sexual immorality

The first and most notorious pitfall for any evangelist is moral failure. I have observed that most evangelists are very passionate men. How else can we explain the zeal to go out into the streets and look like a fool in proclaiming Jesus, often in the midst of great opposition. When those passions are under the control of the Spirit, then great and mighty things can happen. However, these passions can also be captured for evil. Sensuality is a problem for all men, but especially for many evangelists. Why is that? Again, evangelists are passionate people, but let's face it, we see some pretty wicked and sensual things on the street. If you have preached at *Mardi Gras* or a Gay Pride Parade, then you know how debauched the crowds are. You have seen people parading around practically naked. I have seen full-frontal nudity at Gay Pride Parades. Wickedness and perversion abound in these settings. Then there are college football games when the young college women are wearing short dresses.

All of this can work on an evangelist. It is not as though a man sees someone one time and immediately chooses to commit fornication or adultery. It is more like a battering ram used in medieval days where a city was under siege and the invading army kept striking the gate with the battering ram. Eventually the gate gave way and the marauding band entered and wrought havoc. The constant battering ram of scantily clad women and the ubiquitous presence of sexual images can do its work over the long haul. This, of course, is not even mentioning the problem of pornography. Some seventy percent of Evangelical men look at porn at least once per week. And not all porn is equal in wickedness. Some of it starts rather innocuously. Have you noticed the soft porn on Instagram? We all know a desire for porn is insatiable. What one is observing today will not satisfy tomorrow. One will go deeper and deeper into it until he is addicted. He will lose his ministry, or at least he will lack the power of the Spirit in his ministry. And he will likely lose his wife and children. Evil will not be concealed for long (1 Tim. 5:24).

Another reason for the evangelist falling prey to lust is the high-pressure situations he often finds himself in. This can produce a sort of emotional exhalation whenever it is over, causing a loss of inhibition to come over him. It is exactly at this moment when the evangelist becomes prone to lust. His guard is down. There is a kind of elation about the events of the day. It is akin to a construction worker coming home to a cold beer. And then another. And then another. As mentioned, the fact that much of the evangelist's ministry is among the lost, where he is around women of the world—which includes exposure to unchaste language, behavior, and dress—only adds to the problem. The evangelist will be in some of the darkest environments in the world. The evangelist must crucify his flesh each time he evangelizes, and even after he finishes evangelizing. The evangelist must remember that unbelieving women are being led about by Satan, and if Satan can bring about the downfall of an evangelist through some kind of illicit encounter, he will see it as a great victory. That encounter does not have to just be physical, however. If Satan can cause an evangelist to have a dirty thought or desire, he is likewise victorious in his endeavor. The evangelist has to take every possible step to keep himself from stumbling into lust.

This pitfall of moral failure is all too real. Be honest with yourself, are you too involved with any woman who is not your wife? It may only be an emotional attachment at present, but it is still there. It is still adultery. Your sin will be discovered at some point, and you will lose your ministry and probably your family. You must repent now. There is no shame in admitting that you have a problem here. Go to Jesus. Find a trusted brother in the Lord with whom you can share your sin problem. Ask him to pray for you and with you. Ask him to hold you accountable.

Substance abuse

Some men fall prey to substance abuse. It may be alcohol, illegal drugs, or prescription drugs. We all deal with pain in our lives, whether it is physical, emotional, or psychological pain. We are not merely spiritual beings. We have a mind, emotions, and physical lives, all of which can suffer in various ways. We live in a day of instant gratification. We are taught to relieve pain at all costs and as quickly as possible. In times of trauma, people tend to take medication that can be highly addictive. One may suffer from a serious back ailment and the doctor may prescribe an addictive pain killer meant to be used for a short period of time. I have known pastors who got hooked on prescription medication due to serious back issues. They ended up losing their ministries and their good names, bringing shame to the work of Christ.

The root of much evil

Another pitfall is money. I have often said that women and money have ruined more pastors and evangelists than just about anything else. Evangelists are not immune to the pull of the world and materialism. It's very difficult to remove ourselves from its influence. Advertising seems omnipresent, and the harlot of Revelation is constantly calling us away from the work of the gospel to feast on the flesh, the temporal, and the irrelevant. Simply put, stay out of debt. Do not live above your means. If you choose to use a credit card (and let's face it, it is hard to live today, especially to travel, without one) then discipline yourself to pay it off at the end of the month. If at all possible, save your money and pay cash for a car, even if you have to settle for a previously owned car, and even if it is several years old.

We may be stepping on a few toes here, but we believe that the responsibility for providing for one's family falls on the husband, not the wife. We are not saying that a wife cannot work outside the home, especially before the couple has children or after the children are grown. We are saying, however, that the couple ought to live primarily on the husband's salary and save the wife's salary, especially before they have children. Too many couples become accustomed to two incomes and buy a house they can afford on two incomes, but when the wife comes home to care for the children, they get into trouble financially. And financial problems have destroyed many marriages.

Men should not look to their wives to be the bread winner while they do their ministry. Either raise the financial support you need so that you can go full-time in your ministry or continue to work your secular job and evangelize on the side when you are able. I have a friend whose wife was a high powered attorney making a high six figure income. She came home to have children and he was struggling in his sales position. He told me that he thought it was a good idea for his wife, who had a six month old at home, to go back to work. I said, "Not a good idea. First of all, your baby will suffer without your wife's daily care. And second, you will become complacent and find it more and more difficult to grind in your job because you know her salary is a safety net. No, this is on you. You need to make it happen and not look to your wife to bail you out." He agreed and since that time has done quite well.

Because our focus here is on the Reformed evangelist, the reader might assume that money or wealth would not be a temptation. How many Reformed evangelists are wealthy, especially through their ministry? Yet the desire to be rich is no less a temptation for the evangelist as it is for any Christian. The evangelist is actually more prone to such a temptation than most ministers because the evangelist will oftentimes be required to raise his own support. The evangelist will rarely be on a church staff. He will usually not be doing evangelism work full-time. His mind necessarily has to be on finances and donations. Most evangelists forced to work a side job long for the opportunity to have enough money to do evangelism labor full-time. Their thoughts can become consumed with making this happen. Their thoughts might begin to revolve around money instead of Christ. This is something to avoid, since Christ says seek first the kingdom of God and His righteousness, and everything else will be added to you. The evangelist in this case must trust that it is the Lord's will, at least for a season, that he works another job to support his family. If the Lord opens the door at a later time to work as a full-time evangelist, so be it, but if not—so be it.

Likewise, the evangelist who is able to do the work full-time faces temptations when it comes to money. He will typically be living off of donations or the support of churches. But when donations begin to get thin, what is his reaction? Does he panic? Does he lose faith? Does he become obsessive about it? Or on the contrary, when many donors pour into his ministry, what is his reaction? Does he have a thirst for more? Does he use his riches recklessly? Does he get too comfortable? Does his standard of living change? Being rich may be a long shot for the evangelist, which is a blessing. But desiring to be rich is a temptation that all Christians and especially the evangelist will be prone to, whether or not he is a full-time evangelist.

Pride

Another temptation for the evangelist is pride. All Christians are vulnerable to such a vice, but especially in our contemporary context. There is a kind of Christian celebrity-ism afoot in the land. Wanting a seat at the table of Christian popularity is a particularly savage lust. It is rare for evangelists to actually attain such popularity, which is a grace, but the desire to have such a standing is always there. What makes the evangelist especially vulnerable to such a vice is the fact that the evangelist will oftentimes find himself battling many opponents, whether inside or outside the church, so the desire to "prove" himself to others will be very present. He will want to show off for the naysayers. Another vulnerability is the fact that, because the evangelist will oftentimes need financial support, he may do things to "show off" in order to attract more donors.

There is a fine line between sharing with others how the Lord is using you and actually boasting about it. There is a fine line between sharing video of certain evangelistic outreaches for the sake of teaching and accountability and doing so for self-exaltation. Pastors will likewise struggle with such things, but the pastor typically will not have as much of a chip on his shoulder as the evangelist. By virtue of the office of evangelist's fringe status among most Christian circles, he will feel like he has something to prove. This is natural, but can also lead to sinful promotion.

Another area of pride for the evangelist is boasting of conversions. This is somewhat more restrained in the Reformed world due to a healthier understanding of regeneration, but it is something that the evangelist should still watch for. Among open air preachers, this can manifest itself in boasting about crowd sizes or how many people want to kill you. It can manifest itself in how many turnaways you see at the abortion clinic or how many times you have been arrested. This is not to say that mentioning these things is sinful, of course. Sometimes, especially in our culture, the evangelist might indeed be arrested. The open air preacher may see a crowd of frenzied unbelievers. The evangelist may see much fruit is his ministry. To tell others of such things is one thing. Boasting of such scenes is another. Each evangelist will have to evaluate his own heart in this matter.

An Unhealthy Marriage

Most men want to conquer things. When in middle school or high school, most young men pride themselves on their athletic prowess. They gain their identity through their performance on the football field or basketball court. By their early twenties, this begins to morph into gaining their identity in how well they get on with the ladies (we are assuming, of course, that godly young men will sanctify this natural inclination). And by the time men reach their forties, they begin to seek their identity in their job, their position in their profession, how much money they make, and what kind of "toys" they are able to accumulate. If you are like most men, then you pursued diligently the woman you married. Once you "conquered" her and she said "yes," then you moved on to other projects like your job or your ministry.

Men in the ministry can be particularly averse to giving their wives the attention and care they need. They sometimes think that, as long as they provide a roof over their heads and put food on the table and buy the children nice clothes, then they are good to go, that they can spend an inordinate amount of time on their hobbies, job, or ministry. This can be particularly true for evangelists who have a sincere passion for lost souls. Marriages often suffer and die unless the husband gives his wife the care and attention she needs. It goes like this, "Love loss is the fault of the boss, but strife is the fault of the wife." Paul told the Ephesians that husbands are to love their wives as Christ loves the church and gave Himself up for her. This means, of course, that he is to be sacrificial. He is to put his wife's needs ahead of his own. If love is waning in a marriage, then you can be sure that the fault lies with the husband. He is failing to do his job. On the other hand, a marriage of strife, arguing, and shouting at each other is usually the fault of the wife. This isn't always the case, of course, but it generally is. Paul tells the wife to respect her husband. If she is berating him then she is not respecting him. At the end of the day the problems in marriage usually begin with the husband failing to love his wife as he ought. Any woman who is loved sacrificially by her husband will generally delight in following his lead.

Children

Paul tells us that the qualification for being an elder or bishop, among other things, is to manage one's own household well. For if one does not manage his own children, then how can he take care of the church of God (1 Tim. 3:5)? It certainly is true that, at the end of the day, every child of believing parents must be born-again. He or she must repent and believe the gospel. Parents can baptize, catechize, home school, engage in morning and evening family worship, and have their children in church three times per week and make sure they have heard two thousand sermons before going off to college. However, until that child is born-again by a sovereign work of the Holy Spirit, then none of what the parents did is effectual.

Having said this, however, it is also true that parents are to discipline their children biblically. They are to model the

Christian life to their children. They are to love their children and never exasperate them. And they most certainly are never to neglect them or deal harshly with them. It is very difficult for most people to take someone's evangelistic ministry seriously if they know the children are rebellious, have rejected the faith, and gone the way of the world into dissipation.

Bitterness

Perhaps the most subtle temptation for the evangelist will be bitterness. This is a type of sentiment that festers over time, as opposed to all at once. When it comes to the evangelist, bitterness can arise for several reasons. The opposition to the evangelist will come from all sides—the church, his family, the lost, police officers, to name a few. He will also encounter rejection on a regular basis. The truth is, in our culture, rejection to the gospel is a far more prominent experience than faith. If the evangelist is not careful and conscientious about watching against bitterness, it won't be long before such a sentiment overtakes him.

Atheists and nonbelievers are not the only ones who will come against the evangelist. Professing Christians will come against him more than any other group. This is one of the most shocking and tragic realities that every biblical evangelist faces. Professing Christians are often the most persistent mockers of all. They will criticize him regardless of how or what he preaches. This is not to say that every Christian will have such a spirit. Many will come and thank him for preaching the cross. Many will shake his hand or bring him something to drink. But too many Christians will want to yank him down as ferociously as any atheist or Muslim.

This reaction to the public proclamation of the Word has been constant throughout history. The Old Testament prophets' worst foe was the religious establishment of the day. The same was true for Christ. The same happened to Whitefield and Wesley. Professing Christians will question the efficacy of the preaching. They will ask whether Jesus did it this way. They will tell the evangelist that he is not loving enough or that he is too judgmental. They will say that he is pushing sinners further away. In every scenario, the problem comes from the professing Christian not knowing or believing his Bible. Perhaps the professing Christian has never been born-again and thus is no Christian at all. These kinds of grumblers will see the response of the unregenerate world. They will hear the scoffing. Then they will conclude that biblical evangelism must therefore be wrong. They will say that it is harmful. But the evangelist must stick to the Bible for his justification to preach in public, not the world or even the church in such instances. The Bible shows that this kind of response is expected from those dead in sin as well as professing Christians who have not submitted to the Scriptures in this area. It does not mean that the preacher should intentionally antagonize others or look for such a response. He should never intentionally try to look foolish or provoke people's ire. But anyone faithfully proclaiming the Word of God will encounter a stiff-necked and adulterous generation and its typical responses.

This is why the evangelist must expect opposition. He must guard against bitterness. "Jews require a sign, and the Greeks seek after wisdom," but the evangelist must "preach Christ crucified, unto the Jews a stumbling block, and unto the Greeks foolishness" (1 Cor. 1:23). The majority of people exposed to the preaching of Christ will reject it before it reaches their ears. The seed will fall on hard ground (Mt. 13:1–23). The evangelist who presents the beauty of Christ will discover that most are blind and unwilling to look on Him. This is why the professing Christian who does not know his Bible will see open air preaching as harmful or useless. But those who have studied the Bible, especially as it regards evangelism, will realize this kind of response corroborates perfectly with God's promise: "The natural man receiveth not the things of the Spirit of God: for they are foolishness unto him: neither can he know them, because they are spiritually discerned" (1 Cor. 2:14). Again,

"If our gospel be hid, it is hid to them that are lost: in whom the god of this world hath blinded the minds of them which believe not, lest the light of the glorious gospel of Christ, who is the image of God, should shine unto them" (2 Cor. 4:3–4).

Man's greatest problem has always been pride festering in his heart, whether intellectual, physical, monetary, or spiritual. The cross directly confronts him at this point, which is why the cross will always appear foolish. Ancient Athens thought so. Modern college campuses think so. The unbelieving cousin or brother or parent thinks so. Even many churches think so. The evangelist must never forget that the foolishness of preaching is what brings dead men to life. Softening the cross with clever speech or eloquence creates false converts who are drawn to cleverness or eloquence rather than Christ. Trying to meet the unbeliever on neutral ground can only lead to the further hardening of his heart, justifying his rebellion against God. The evangelist must proclaim Christ and Him crucified. He must stick to the foolishness of preaching and the gospel. God has always used humble means to save dead souls because in doing so He gets all the glory. And when the world turns on the evangelist, he must remain tender and patient.

Bad Health

Paul tells Timothy to discipline himself for the purpose of godliness (1 Tim. 4:7). He goes on to say that bodily discipline is of some benefit. An evangelist must be able to curb his appetite for food and drink. Paul tells us that we are not to be mastered by anything (1 Cor. 6:12). Not only does overeating and poor hygiene look bad for the evangelist, it can be very harmful to his health and leads to a myriad of problems which can take him away from fruitful ministry. I often tell young preachers that they need to find some kind of exercise regimen which works for them. Perhaps it is *CrossFit*, cycling, running, swimming, basketball, walking, or some other form of conditioning program. But they need to begin in their twenties or thirties so that the habit of regular exercise becomes a part of their lives. While men are young, their bodies are pretty forgiving and they can get away with eating too much and getting very little exercise. However, by their late thirties or early forties, their metabolism slows down, and taking in more calories than they are burning is a recipe for weight gain and poor health. I have friends in the ministry who never acquired an exercise program and now are grossly overweight, and their bodies are breaking down. They are constantly sick, lethargic, depressed, and unable to give much energy to their ministries, and this was all avoidable if they had purposed to exercise regularly and to eat well.

Laziness

In a way, this is a temptation to any gospel minister, especially those who have been in the same ministry for a long time. But the temptation will be different for pastors than it will be for the evangelists. For instance, if a pastor gets lazy in the study, it will show in his sermon on Sunday. If it persists for a long period of time, the flock will become disgruntled. Perhaps he will be called before the elders or congregation. He could potentially lose his ministry at the church. In other words, there is an element of accountability that is involved in the pastoral ministry. The same would be true if the pastor becomes lazy in his visitations or prayer life. It will be reflected in how he handles himself before the congregation and, typically, there will be repercussions.

For the evangelist, however, this layer of accountability is not always there. Ideally, the evangelist will evangelize with at least one other person whenever he goes out, but that is not always the case. The evangelist will be more tempted to "wing it." After all, because he encounters a different group or person when he goes out with the gospel, he can typically provide the same material to each respective group. The same is true for the evangelist who does pulpit supply at different congregations. He can preach the same sermon over and over again. This is not to say that this approach is wrong. It is to say that, as a consequence of this situation, the evangelist may not feel the need to study on a regular basis. He may become lax in his preparation time. The evangelist has to guard against this. Like any minister, the evangelist must be a person of prayer and regular study. Study will provide the evangelist with an ongoing supply of material to bring to the lost, but even more importantly, it will keep his own soul warm towards the things of God. Theological study should be an act of devotion first and foremost, so to neglect such a means of grace will cause the soul to grow dull and insensitive.

Mental health

We are not merely spiritual beings. We have a physical body which can become ill. We have emotions which can disintegrate into major problems. And our minds can become sick due to stress, lack of sleep, guilt, or any number of other contributing factors. Some men are more prone to depression than others. We have known godly men (Charles Spurgeon and Jonathan Edwards, for example) who have battled depression for many years. In a time of great physical exhaustion and a sense of desertion, the great Welsh preacher Martin Lloyd-Jones became severely depressed for a season. He checked himself into a hospital for about a month and had several bouts with the devil while in the hospital. He eventually came out the other side with great victory and joy, but the reality of this dark night of the soul ravaged him severely for a season. Never underestimate the potential in your own life for mental duress and failure. Guard your mind and emotions as you would your personal identity. Do not allow the devil to steal it from you.

Satan, the great deceiver

Beware of Satan and his minions which seek to do you harm. Peter refers to the devil as a roaring lion who roams about, looking for someone to devour. One of the devil's favorite approaches is to tempt the believer to sin against God's grace. It goes like this. The devil "speaks" to the Christian, saying, "Go ahead and go after that woman. After all, your wife does not respect you. You deserve a little fun and excitement in your life. Besides, all you need to do after being with that woman is to confess your sin and you know God will forgive you. After all, God's grace is greater than your sin." But once you go down that road, then the devil becomes the accuser of the brethren and says something like this, "It is all over for you now. God could never accept you back. You are lost forever. You are a hypocrite, and you know God hates hypocrites. So, give up this notion of Christianity. It may work for others, but it certainly is not working for you." And when you sin, the tendency is to go light on your sin, to tell yourself that this is really not that big of a deal after all, that you can continue to live this way without incrimination. But when this happens, you have grieved the Holy Spirit, and when you grieve Him, you lose His power and presence in your life. At that point, you are opening yourself up for greater temptation and eventual compromise. You are then on your way to spiritual shipwreck of your faith.

Every ministry comes with certain dangers and temptations. The office of evangelist is no exception. The best way to defend against dangers and temptations is to know exactly how they may come at you. The worst way to defend against dangers and temptations is to remain unconscious or skeptical of them. This is why it is imperative to spend ample time on this topic. The evangelist must walk with wisdom at all hours of the day, not just when in the battle. In fact, the most opportune time for the enemy to take down the evangelist is not while he is engaged in evangelism, but when he is not. This chapter will mention several additional examples of dangers and temptations, along with ways to guard against them.

Remedies to
Avoid Pitfalls

How are we to live out the Bible's commands to watch over our hearts, to pay close attention to ourselves and our doctrine, and to allow the word of God to dwell richly within us? We will mention three important exercises. The first is meditation, then adoration, and then supplication. What do I mean by these things?

Biblical meditation

Let's look briefly at the spiritual discipline of meditation. Consider these words from Moses to Joshua. "This book of the law shall not depart out of your mouth but you shall meditate on it day and night, so that you may be careful to do according to all that is written in it; for then you will make your way prosperous, and then you will have success" (Joshua 1:8). Do you drink in the word of God, allowing it to feed and strengthen your heart and soul? Or do you gargle it like mouthwash and spit it out of your mouth?

The Bible on many occasions puts forth the virtue of meditation. As Joshua prepared to lead the sons of Israel into the
Promised Land, he was told several times to be strong and
courageous. Yahweh said that wherever Joshua put his feet,
He would give him the land, that no man would be able to
stand before him, that he would have success (conquering his
enemies) wherever he went as long as he did not turn from
God's path for him, as long as he meditated on the book of
the law (Joshua 1:3-9). The book of the law obviously refers
to the Bible they had at the time; the five books of Moses, the
Pentateuch. In a similar fashion, David says that the man who
does not walk in the counsel of the wicked, who does not stand
in the path of sinners, who does not sit in the seat of scoffers (in
other words, one who does not allow himself to be adversely
affected by heresy or worldly wisdom), but who meditates on
God's law both day and night (drinking it as a way of life, not
gargling it) will be like a tree firmly planted by streams of water,
which yields its fruit in its season. He will be like a leaf of a
tree that does not whither, that whatever this man does he will
prosper (Psalm 1:1-3).

At one of the low points of his life, while in a state of utter
desperation in the wilderness, King David says, "When I
remember Thee on my bed, I meditate on Thee in the night
watches." It is because of this meditation that he then says, "For
Thou hast been my help, and in the shadow of Thy wings I sing
for joy" (Psalm 63:6-7). In another time of great upheaval,
David also says, "Tremble, and do not sin; meditate in your
heart upon your bed, and be still. Offer the sacrifices of righteousness, and trust in the Lord" (Psalm 4:4-5). He closes
this Psalm with great expectation of comfort and deliverance,
saying, "Thou hast put gladness in my heart, more than when
their grain and new wine abound. In peace I will both lie down
and sleep, for Thou alone, O Lord, dost make me to dwell in
safety" (Psalm 4:7-8). Asaph says something similar, "I will
remember my song in the night; I will meditate with my heart,

and my spirit ponders (or searches)" (Psalm 77:6). He ends by affirming his confidence in Yahweh's protection and provision, that He will lead them like a flock (Psalm 77:20).

David, in his masterful Psalm on the power, profundity, and purity of God's word says, "O how I love Thy law! It is my meditation all the day" (Psalm 119:97). From his delight in meditating on God's law, David goes on to say that His commandments make him wiser than all his enemies, give him more insight than all his teachers, more wisdom than the aged, restrains him from sin, and keeps him on the narrow way of holiness (Psalm 119:98-104).

What do we mean by meditation? I do not mean *Transcendental Meditation,* which merely vacates the mind. In fact, Biblical meditation is just the opposite. It is a filling of the mind and heart with God's word. It is like a cow chewing its cud—the cow chews the grass, digests it, and then vomits it, and chews on it again. Biblical meditation is bringing up any portion of Scripture that has been memorized or recently read, and chewing on it some more. We are thus to ruminate on God's holy, inerrant, inspired, and infallible word.

If we have more solid Evangelical books than ever, if we have such great preachers and ready access to their sermons through the internet, if we have such fine theological institutions and such wonderfully trained pastors, why then, do we lack power? We have the electrical wiring, as it were, the structure for power, but we lack the juice! If our people say that they believe in the lostness of mankind without Christ, that these people will go to hell for eternity if they do not repent and believe the gospel, then why do so few of us make a practice of sharing our faith? If we have our books on Christian marriage and our weekend seminars on how to fulfill our Biblical roles better, why then does the Evangelical church have as many divorces as the secular world? If Jesus is more powerful than Islam, if He is more powerful than secularism, if He is more powerful than materialism, then why has Islam conquered the Middle East and North

Africa? Why has secularism won the day in Europe? Why is materialism the god of America, even within the church? The answer, my friend, is that we approach the Bible as a mere book, we embrace the Bible as mere doctrine, but we do not experience its life-changing power. We gargle it but we don't drink it. Biblical meditation seeks to imbibe the Word of God.

This life-changing power, this transforming work of Christ, comes as you take in God's word, as you saturate your mind and heart with it; but it also comes to fruition as you take time every day—as you drive to work, as you walk or run for exercise, as you lay down at night before you sleep and think on the word of God. You are to be mighty in the word of God, and this comes through belief in the power of the Holy Spirit to energize you. Most of the great preachers in history have been masterful meditators on God's word. This was the secret of their power in the pulpit. Charles Spurgeon saturated his mind with God's word, thought deeply about it all week, and then prepared his Sunday morning sermon late Saturday night or even Sunday morning. George Whitefield spent hours meditating on God's word as his horse took him to his next preaching appointment. Whitefield then stood and preached extemporaneously for an hour or two at a time. Archibald Alexander, the great Princeton theologian, spent hours each week meditating on a passage and without concern for crafting phrases, would simply stand, open his mouth, and divine eloquence of unusual saving and sanctifying power came forth.

We must regain the heart of Jesus in life and ministry. Enough of sterile sermons, lifeless small group meetings, passionless preaching and public worship, and preoccupation with personal peace and affluence while the world languishes in darkness. Fill up your mind and heart daily with the life changing power of God's holy word, and then see what He does in you and through you as an evangelist.

Adoration

But then we must also engage regularly in adoration. The Bible is replete with references to adoration, and as an evangelist, you must make this your regular practice. Consider Revelation 4:11, "Worthy art Thou, our Lord and our God, to receive glory, honor, and power, for Thou didst create all things, and because of Thy will they existed, and were created." We are to rejoice in the Lord always. We are to consider everything joy when we encounter various trials. We are to have a song of praise in our mouths, for God has lifted us from the miry clay and has put us on a solid rock. From Genesis to Revelation, we find the people of God giving praise and adoration to their great King and Savior. Abraham offered sacrifices to God (Gen. 12:7, 13:4, 18, 22:9). So did Isaac and Jacob (Gen. 26:25, 28:18). Moses, when seeing the bush burn but not consumed, heard the voice of God say, "Take off your shoes for the place you are standing is holy ground" (Ex. 3:5). God later gave explicit directions on how He was to be worshiped in the building of the tabernacle (Ex. 25-31). After witnessing the awesome destruction of the Egyptian army by drowning in the Red Sea, the people of God sang a song of praise to their mighty deliverer (Ex. 15). The glory of God in the form of a cloud hovered over the tabernacle and the people bowed down to worship Him (Ex. 40). Joshua met the captain of the Lord's host and was told the same thing as Moses— "Take off your shoes. The place where you are standing is holy ground" (Josh. 5:13-15). When Sisera fled from Barak and hid in the tent of Jael and she drove the tent peg through his head, the people sang praises to the God who had delivered them from oppression (Judges 5). And of course, much of David's praise and adoration is found in his Psalms. Solomon praised the Lord (1 Kings 8:22ff).

We also see praise and humble, joyful adoration given to Yahweh by the prophets. In one of the more remarkable examples of the Lord Jesus giving adoration to His Father, when seeing the hardness of heart of the religious leaders and the willingness of the poor to receive Him, He says, "I praise Thee, Father, Lord of heaven and earth, that Thou hast hidden these things from the wise and intelligent and hast revealed them to infants. Yes, Father, for this way was well pleasing in Thy sight" (Mat. 11:25-26). And the Apostle Paul, in the midst of instruction, often bursts forth into praising God, seemingly unable to control himself, becoming lost in praise and wonder at the great mercy and grace of God (Rom. 11:33-36, 1 Tim. 1:17). And we repeatedly find the four living creatures, the twenty-four elders, and myriads of angels giving praise and adoration to the Lord Jesus, the Lion of the tribe of Judah, the root of David, the bright and morning star, the Faithful Witness, the first born from the dead, the ruler of the kings of the earth, the One who has loved us, who has released us from our sins by His blood (Rev. 1, 4, 5).

And why is it that these great saints of Biblical antiquity find the praise of God constantly on their lips? They seem to understand powerfully what we too often take for granted—all they have, all they are, every aspect of their eternal salvation is by God's mercy and grace. They understood that they had a cobra heart (Psalm 58:1-5), that they loved sin and hated God, that consequently they lived a godless life and had a filthy past (Rom. 3:10ff). They came to know that they were under the very wrath of God, that they had no hope, that they were without God in this world (Ephesians 2:12). They came to understand they lived a poisonous life, that like an herbicide sprayed on crops in a field kills everything on which it lands, their relationships were destroyed (James 3:2-12), that all their religious or moral efforts to conquer their sin problem were to no avail. But God came to them in the person and work of the Holy Spirit (Eph. 1:13-14). He brought someone to them who preached Jesus and Him crucified. The Spirit caused them to be born-again, to have the heart of Jesus that loves God and hates sin, that applied the pure, precious, and undefiled blood of Jesus to their souls, that washed away all their sins, that gave them the very righteousness of Jesus Christ (Rom. 5:1-8, Col. 1:13-14), that gave them the holiness of Jesus (1 Cor. 1:30) that enabled them to walk in holiness, to obey the law of God (Ezek. 36:27). They, along with Isaiah, after seeing the three-fold holiness of God, came to understand the depth of their sin and cried out to God, "Woe is me, I am undone" (Isa. 6:1ff). In the light of God's holiness, Isaiah came to see that it was as though he was a decomposing body in a tomb. He was utterly and completely annihilated. But God had mercy on him, on the others, and they consequently could not help but give continuous praise to God.

Why then, my friend, do we tend to go through our days grumbling, cold-hearted, and complaining about how our spouses, children, parents, or employers treat us? I am not unaware that sorrow often comes our way. Jesus wept and so do we at the loss of loved ones. James tells us to consider everything as joy (James 1:2-4), but later he tells us to be miserable, to mourn, to weep, to let our laughter be turned to sorrow and our joy to gloom (James 4:9). Paul tells us to rejoice in the Lord always (Phil. 3:1, 4:4) but earlier in the same epistle, he tells us that he wept over those in the church who actually were enemies of the cross of Christ (Phil. 3:18). The glory, the mystery of the Christ-centered life, is the complementarity of truth. Jesus is fully God, and He is fully man. The Bible is the word of God, but it is recorded, written down by man. God chooses people to be saved before the foundation of the world (Ephesians 1:4-5), but everyone who calls on the name of the Lord will be saved (Rom. 10:13). And so it with us in joy and sorrow! We are to rejoice always, and we are to weep and mourn over our sin and the sin and suffering we find in the world. Only the true Christian can do both.

So, you are to live a life of constant adoration and praise to God. This will keep you in good stead as an evangelist. Step back, my friends, and see what great things God has wrought for you in your eternal salvation! Indeed, you were without hope, you were without God in this world, but you who were far off have been brought near by the blood of Jesus. Yes, rejoice in the Lord. Again I say rejoice in the Lord!

Biblical supplication

And finally, as an evangelist you need to practice the Biblical discipline of supplication. Consider this word from Daniel, "So I gave my attention to the Lord God to seek Him by prayer and supplications, with fasting, sackcloth and ashes" (Dan. 9:3). After reading the prophet Jeremiah and having known of the promised return from the exile, Daniel seeks Yahweh with diligence and zeal—fasting, putting on sackcloth and ashes, and making supplication. Paul tells us to pray with supplication (Phil. 4:6). Zechariah records God promising that He will pour forth a Spirit of grace and supplication so that they will look on Jesus, whom they had pierced (Zech.12:10).

We likewise are to make supplications to God. But what does this word mean? It has the idea of urgent, fervent, persistent prayer grounded upon an intolerable burden. We see this in the life of our Lord Jesus who, in the days of His flesh, offered up both prayers and supplications with loud crying and tears to the One able to save Him from death, and He was heard because of His piety (Heb. 5:7). We see it in Isaiah, who with great emotion cries out to the Lord, "O that Thou wouldst rend the heavens and come down, that the mountains may quake at Thy presence" (Isa. 64:1ff). We see it in David, who prayed in like manner in a time of great darkness, "Give ear to my words, O Lord. Consider my groaning. Heed the sound of my cry for help, my King and my God, for to Thee do I pray" (Psalm 5:1-2). We see this intolerable burden in Nehemiah who, when hearing that the people were in distress and reproach, that the walls of the city of Jerusalem were still broken down after all those years of dwelling again in the land of Judah, sat down, wept, and mourned for days, fasting and praying before the God of heaven (Neh. 1:3-4). We see it further displayed in Nehemiah when he heard that, after all Yahweh had done for them; the people repaid His beneficence by continuing to give their children to be married to pagans. He contended with them and cursed them and struck some of them and pulled out their hair, and made them swear to God, "You shall not give your daughters to their sons, nor take their daughters for your sons or for yourselves" (Neh. 13:23-24).

My friends—all of our evangelistic activity, all of our planning, all of our strategizing, all of our money, all of our buildings will be powerless until we gain an intolerable burden, until we learn to pray prayers of supplication. Business as usual will not work. The church in the west is losing the war. Okay, we have a few oases in the desert of the western church. We have a few bright spots, but we are losing ground. We are experiencing a net loss of 3,500 churches per year in America and that, by 2050, only 11% of Americans will attend church at least twice per month. Your church may be growing financially, numerically, and even spiritually. That is, you may be seeing your people truly growing in the grace and knowledge of the Lord Jesus, but unless you are seeing many, many conversions—unless men, women, and children are joining your church by profession of faith in great numbers—then your church is already dying. A married couple which does not produce children will see their legacy die with them. If your church is merely growing through transfer of membership, then you are kidding yourself. You are prolonging the inevitable, like many in places of power in our country which think we can continue to spend more than we take in. It is mindless! We are destined to failure. So it is within the church. We have lost the day on the homosexual agenda. Little or no progress has been made in the abolition of abortion. Corruption in government abounds. More and more laws are needed to hold our debauchery in check. Mosques are being built every year in America. Supposedly well-educated and informed people speak of the virtues of Islam, asking us to co-exist, simply to get along, while these same people blindly ignore the degradation of women in the Muslim culture. Islam has never been willing to co-exist with any other religion. It is within the DNA of Islam only to conquer. Do you want to see your children and grand-children living under Shariah law? Do you think I am writing in hyperbole? Augustine could never have dreamed that his beloved North Africa would be Muslim within four hundred years of his death, and yet it was.

My dear friends, until you gain an intolerable burden over how depraved and godless we are, until you see how powerless and hopeless we are to avert the coming judgment of God on our nation, then you will foolishly continue on with business as usual. You will be like Nero, who fiddled while Rome burned.

How do you gain this intolerable burden to supplicate with passion, zeal, and persistence before the King of Glory? You must get a fresh glimpse of Christ's power and authority. You must get something of the zeal you find in Jesus when He cleansed the temple (John 2:13-19), driving out the money changers because they had made the court of the Gentiles, the place where the Jews were to pray for the nations (Isa. 56:7), into a robber's den (Jer. 7:11). Jesus' actions were premeditated. He had been coming to the temple for years. The action of these greedy men was nothing new. Jesus made a whip and drove them out, turning the tables over as He made His way through the temple, coins flying in every direction, men fleeing from His presence, animals running for refuge. His disciples later remembered what David had said, "For zeal for Thy house has consumed me, and the reproaches of those who reproach Thee have fallen on me" (Psalm 69:9). Will you gain a fresh vision of the glory, authority, and zeal of Christ for His kingdom? Will you supplicate with passion and loud crying like the Lord Jesus? Will you learn to pray in the Spirit (Eph. 6:18), praying until you pray, experiencing the felt presence of God, finding unusual felicity in the speech of prayer, praying with divine eloquence, like a preacher under the anointing of the Spirit as he preaches the gospel with convicting, converting power!

Enough of business as usual! Enough of our passionless orthodoxy! True Christian faith is lived in the heart, not merely in the mind; and when this occurs, it will manifest itself in life. We will pray and live with Spirit power that will tear down the strongholds of the devil, that will see countless thousands in our communities suddenly arrested, convicted, and crying out, "What must we do to be saved?" Do you believe that God can do this in our nation again? Do you believe that He will? Are you willing, faithful evangelist, to pay the price to see this happen? It shall not come without supplication, without the intolerable burden of Daniel, Nehemiah, and Jesus.

PART 4

Advice for Churches

14

Advice for Churches— Evaluation and Examination

W hat advice can we give the church for making use of the evangelists God gives them in their local church? We will approach this issue with several key components—evaluation, examination, and training and sending. These components will be broken up into two chapters.

Evaluation

We have already observed that many of our Reformed churches are woefully weak in evangelistic outreach. Here we will go more deeply into the matter. One of the major tenets of any leadership principle is to evaluate or assess where you are at the present time. We are now appealing to pastors, evangelists, elders, or deacons in the church. Be honest with yourself and your fellow church officers. Are you a growing church? Are you an evangelistically-minded church? Now please understand that I am not suggesting numerical growth is the most important metric available. Plenty of cults and progressive churches are growing numerically. However, numerical growth should not be altogether rejected as a legitimate evaluating device. After all, Luke tells us how many people were saved at Pentecost and how many people were in the church a few days later.

If a church is not growing numerically, then we should at least entertain the question of why not, particularly in the western world, where there is very little persecution or opposition to the gospel. At our children's birthdays each year, my wife and I would stand them up against the door frame of their bedroom door and measure their height, comparing it to the last time we measured it one year earlier. Physical growth is natural for children. If you have a ten year old who has not grown in height in a year or two, then you are rightly concerned for his health.

Surely, we can use the same observation for the church. A healthy church should be growing numerically. But how should the church be growing numerically? If a local congregation is preaching the word of God and rightly administering the sacraments of baptism and the Lord's supper, if it observes Biblical worship, if it has godly leadership by her pastors, elders, deacons, and evangelists, and if it has members who love Jesus, then surely there ought to be some amount of transfer growth into the church. We should expect at least a few people in the community to be drawn to the church.

We can also go further in our evaluation of the church. Is the local congregation growing by conversion growth? We realize we are not living in the midst of a revival culture in today's western church. We also know of the increased secularization of our culture, and some areas of the United States are very liberal and secular in their view of the world and their disdain for Christianity. At the same time, we believe that God has His elect in every city and that we should be seeing some people come to faith in Christ, be baptized, and join the local congregation. We also readily acknowledge that not all people whom we see call on the name of the Lord to be saved will join our congregations. Sometimes there are sociological or cultural issues affecting dress, style of worship, or standards of living which make some people uncomfortable in attending and joining our churches. But can we not agree that we should be seeing people each year come to faith in Christ, be baptized, and join our churches, and then give evidence of spiritual growth in gospel holiness and living out a Biblical worldview?

I once added up every dollar amount my former denomination spent on church budgets, building programs, and giving to world missions for one year. I then divided the number of adult professions of faith for that one year into the total giving number. I was astonished to find that one adult profession of faith cost around $158,000 each. And actually, the number in all the churches in America is ten times greater. Surely you will agree with me that something is amiss.

So we must ask you, pastor, elder, deacon, evangelist, or interested church member—how many adult professions of faith did you have last year, and how many of those people joined your congregation and are active, growing participants in the life of your congregation? If there are very few, and if your congregation is like most Reformed ones in America, then the answer is, indeed, "not many." This should surely grieve you. If you have very few conversions and it doesn't bring heartache to you and, at the very least, move you to ask, "Why is this true about us," then we are very concerned for you. Don't simply play the "election card." That's when people say, "Well, God chooses people to be His and I have nothing to do with that. If there are no elect, then this is not my problem." Remember that, after laying down very clearly the doctrine of election in Romans 8:28-31 and Romans 9:14-18, Paul then says in Romans 10:1, "Brethren, my heart's desire and my prayer to God for them is for their salvation." God is sovereign in all things, including the salvation of the elect, but at the same time we are expected to respond with faith to the gospel and to go with the gospel to the lost. We see this played out further in Romans 10:11-17:

For the Scripture says, "Whoever believes in Him will not be put to shame." For there is no distinction between Jew and Greek; for the same Lord is Lord of all, abounding in riches for all who call on Him; for "Everyone who calls on the name of the Lord will be saved."

How then are they to call on Him in whom they have not believed? How are they to believe in Him whom they have not heard? And how are they to hear without a preacher? But how are they to preach unless they are sent? Just as it is written: "How beautiful are the feet of those who bring good news of good things!" However, they did not all heed the good news; for Isaiah says, "Lord, who has believed our report?" So faith comes from hearing, and hearing by the word of Christ.

Paul is unequivocal here. The sovereignty of God and human responsibility are both at play in the work of evangelism. God has His elect, and our job is to go out into the world and find them. This raises the question, then—why are most Reformed churches woeful when it comes to evangelism? Why do very few of our churches hardly see any adult professions of faith? There are three major gifts every church needs if it is to be a faithful, well balanced ministry. The first are speaking gifts like teaching, prophesying, leading, or exhorting. The second is a gift of serving, giving, and showing mercy (Rom. 12:6-8). The third is the gift of evangelism (2 Tim. 4:5).

The imbalance in Reformed communities

Most Reformed churches are heavy on teaching but weak on evangelistic and mercy ministry. Perhaps the reason for this is that we attract pastors who love to study theology. We love to read the Puritans, Calvin, Edwards, Martin Lloyd-Jones, John MacArthur, and R.C. Sproul. And of course, this is very good. We need solid Reformed and Biblical theology. And our churches tend to attract members who love the same thing.

Consequently, our pastors, elders, and deacons tend to focus on the exposition of the Scriptures and making sure their people are well trained in correct theology. Evangelism tends to take a back seat to the church's teaching ministry. When this occurs, then the church will tend to be sterile. By this we mean at least two things. First, they are sterile in that they are unable to reproduce. They rarely find people becoming new believers, being born-again through their ministries. And second, they are sterile because they rarely attract "unwashed" people into their churches. They rarely see people from the world, people who are drug addicts, prostitutes, gang bangers, homeless, and others come to faith and join their churches. They tend to be a well-educated, professional, bookish, white collar kind of membership.

On the other hand, some churches are heavy on evangelism but light on teaching. I am thinking now of what I call mega-mega churches. Just about every major city in the United States has at least one of them. Many such churches can boast of thousands of people attending ten or twelve campuses throughout the region, with each location tied in by technology to watch the lead pastor, as they call him, preach to all the campuses at the same time. It's a stretch to say that they are truly evangelistic in practice, but for the sake of argument, I will grant that they are. However, they are weak in teaching, and when this happens in a church, then it will be a shallow church. Perhaps many people are coming to faith, but they are failing to grow in gospel holiness and their knowledge of God and His attributes. They will also produce a vast number of false converts.

There are still other churches which have a genuine burden and concern for the weak, the oppressed, the poor. This is good too. Every church is to minister to the least of these in our communities. However, a church which is strong in mercy ministry but weak in teaching and evangelism will soon become a social gospel church. Their concern for the poor is not balanced with a concern for their souls and it is not informed by what the

Scriptures say concerning the nature of all unregenerate people in our world.

The bottom line is that we must have all three of these gifts working simultaneously if we are to be a Biblical and therefore well-balanced church. So how do you assess your church at this present time? Would you say you are heavy on teaching but light on mercy ministry or evangelism? It is important we honestly assess where we are. Only then can you as a church leader strive to make necessary changes toward a more balanced ministry.

There is one last thing to consider in the evaluation process. You will not alter the status quo in your church unless you have a "holy dissatisfaction" with where you are presently. Are you growing numerically, at least by a few people every year? Or are you seeing very few conversions? Do these realities concern you? Are you grieved by them? Do you lack a passion for souls? Do you really see multitudes falling into hell every day all around the world? What will you do to address the situation? Do you as a church or individual have a problem in this regard?

Examination

This leads to the second component—examination. By this we mean an examination of Scripture. What does the Bible say about our responsibility to reach the nations, including our own nation and communities, with the gospel of Jesus Christ? Let's get past our traditions and go *ad fontes*, back to the sources. That source, of course, is the Bible. I am sure you remember the wrist bracelet which was so popular a number of years ago, "WWJD?". What would Jesus do is not really the question we should be concerning ourselves with. Instead, we should ask, "What did He do?" And whatever Jesus did in ministry is what we should do. So, consider the following in the life and ministry of our Lord Jesus.

During His early Galilean ministry, Jesus sent out His twelve disciples in pairs to proclaim the Kingdom of God (the new eschatological kingdom of peace, power, redemption, and reconciliation). Afterwards, He resolutely set His face toward Jerusalem and began to move in a southernly direction, eventually to offer Himself up as the atoning sacrifice for the sins of all His people. It is at this point that He gave the seventy a mission. They were to go before Him into southern Galilee and find people in the various towns and villages (there perhaps were as many as one hundred and fifty of them) who were receptive to the message of the Kingdom of God. They went in pairs, probably to give them some measure of security and encouragement. They were to take no money, no shoes, no nothing. Why? Perhaps to remind them that their Heavenly Father would provide for them, but also because they could better identify with those whom they would see, the poor and the downtrodden. They were to go directly to the towns and villages, suggesting they were to go in haste and not waste time. And they were to look for the men of peace. If one was there, then they were to pronounce peace upon that man and his household and to minister to those in the man's household.

Who were these men of peace for whom the thirty-five pairs of disciples were searching? They were people who were open to the message of the Kingdom of God. We know this because Jesus told His disciples to shake the dust from their feet if they were rejected, and to announce that judgment was coming due to their unresponsiveness. It appears that the disciples spent at least one night in each town (Jesus told them to accept food and lodging from men of peace). So, assuming they spent two days and one night in each town, each pair could visit two to three towns per week (they would not have traveled on the Sabbath). Within three or four weeks, the seventy could have visited all of the villages and towns in that region. Luke tells us that the seventy came back to Jesus filled with joy, saying that even the demons were subject to them in His name (verse 17). Indeed, the kingdom of this world was becoming the kingdom of our Lord and of His Christ (Rev. 11:15).

It should be obvious by now that business as usual is not

working. The Evangelical church in the United States is generally and exceedingly weak, compromised, lethargic, lukewarm, and dying. What must we do? We must gain a passion for souls to be saved. And then what? We need a method of reaching lost souls in our communities. First, how do we gain a passion for souls? If you have never had such a passion, then perhaps the first thing you must do is answer this question—are you sure you are a Christian? Those who have been delivered from the domain of darkness and transferred into the kingdom of God cannot stop speaking what they have seen and heard. To be sure, we all lose our zeal from time to time, but if you have never known a zeal for the lost, then you very well may be spiritually dead. Therefore, repent of your sins, confess Jesus Christ as Lord, call upon Him to save you, and then the Spirit will give you a zeal to open your mouth and proclaim the excellencies of Him who called you from darkness to light. If you have known that zeal in the past but have grown cold hearted, then you must repent of this great evil. Is this too strong a word—great evil? Not at all. To have the pearl of great price and to refuse to offer it to those in need is the height of pride, selfishness, and greed. Confess your sin and cling to Jesus for His grace and power. And then remember what you were like before your conversion and think on all the mighty things God has done in your life, not only in saving you but also in providing for your needs and sustaining you in all your heartaches of this life.

But then what? What is our method of reaching people? What did Jesus and the Apostles do? Doesn't it make sense to study what Jesus and the Apostles did and then try to put it into practice? We have written extensively in the past on the vital necessity of public preaching and evangelism, as well as pastors preaching regularly on evangelistic themes to their congregations. Every pastor ought to give an opportunity in every sermon for people to repent and call on the name of the Lord to be saved. Evangelistic preaching in the church and on the street is the foundation, but intentional evangelism to neighbors, coworkers, family, and strangers you meet during the day is also vital. What's more, the two work together. Open air preaching is like the carpet bombing the Allies used in World War II over Germany and the Pacific islands. It softened up the enemy, but ground troops were still essential, going from town to town, street to street, door-to-door to root out and conquer the Nazis in Europe and the Japanese in the Pacific. Likewise, the ground game is essential to reach our communities for Christ. We must go and share Christ unto them. You must die to your fear of rejection, your fear of man, and your fleshly desire to be at ease in Zion. Are you willing to do so this very moment?

And how did Jesus tell His disciples to evangelize? In Matthew 10, He sent His twelve disciples out in pairs. We know this because of how Matthew constructs the wording—Andrew and Peter, James and John, Phillip, and Bartholomew. They were to look for houses of peace. It was in those households where the good news of the gospel could take root. Later on, in sending out the seventy, Jesus gave them the same technique. They were not to waste their time on people who were resistant. They were to go to those whom the Father had chosen before the foundation of the world and in whom the Spirit was working. We tend to spend far too much time on hard soil, rocky soil, and weed infested soil, instead of good soil.

As an example of how to reach your neighbors, consider what I have been doing in my neighborhood. Wini and I have been praying for that neighborhood. Specifically, we have been praying for the Holy Spirit to lead us to people of peace. Then I have been walking through the neighborhood, speaking either to people I see on their porch or in their yard, or knocking on their door. And here's what I am saying: "My name is Al Baker. My wife, Wini, and I live across the road from you. We have been wanting to meet our neighbors and find out if there are ways we can serve our community better. I am wondering if there is anything we can pray for you about? Or, to put it another way, if you could ask God for a miracle, what would it be? We have seen God do amazing things in our lives. The most amazing thing God has done for us is to bring us to Himself. I was far away from God until He showed me my sin and gave me the grace to call upon Him to forgive my sins and to give me peace. I am wondering, do you have a similar story?"

It never ceases to amaze me how many people will open up and tell me their trials. One man I spoke with lives by himself and can hardly walk. Another man told me that his wife is in early stages of Alzheimers. Another said she needs friends. I was able to pray specifically for each of these people. And then I say, "We also are interested in having what we call a Discovery Group where we plan to read the Bible and find out what God has to say about how we can find peace, purpose, and power in our lives. Is that something you would be interested in doing?" We are finding that most of the people are very interested in such a group.

Church attendance has been dwindling for years. Thom Rainer believes that, after the Coronavirus pandemic, as much as twenty percent of church attenders will not return. This is quite easy to explain. For at least thirty years the Evangelical church has become event driven and entertainment based, especially with contemporary Christian music and mega-church celebrity pastors and programs out the wazoo. So, when public worship shut down, the people stayed home and live-streamed their favorite worship service and pastor. Then the people began to say to themselves, "Wait, this is easy. No hassle. I can sleep in, relax, drink my coffee, lounge around in my pjs, watch my favorite service, and then watch the NFL games all afternoon."

So, here's our great opportunity to do what Jesus did. People need Christian fellowship and study. Should we not make a concerted, intentional effort to reach out to our neighbors? By this I do not mean "friendship" evangelism. You are always to be friendly to all people, especially your neighbors. I am talking about doing what Jesus and His apostles did, going directly to people, looking for those who are open, who are people of peace, and then minister the gospel to them. Don't waste your time on people who are hard-hearted or not interested. Look for the people of peace. They are there. They are the elect of God from eternity past. Seek to minister the gospel to them.

The seventy came back from their mission, joyfully telling Jesus all that happened. You will have the same joy. There is a certain joy and expectancy in seeing God at work before your very eyes. I promise that, if you will venture out of your comfort zone, you will be amazed at what God does, how He leads you to people who really want Jesus and all that He offers us in His person and work.

The example of Paul

And then, consider the ministry of the great Apostle Paul as a template for how you should move forward in your church. What did Paul do after his dramatic conversion on the road to Damascus as he went to arrest and imprison Christian believers there? Without question, the Apostle Paul believed in the doctrine of the sovereignty of God in everything (1 Thes. 5:18), including the electing grace of God in salvation (Rom. 8:28-30, Rom. 9:14-18, Eph. 1:3-6). His belief in the sovereignty of God (that God foreordains whatsoever comes to pass), however, did nothing to mitigate his zeal for going far, fast, and furious with the gospel. While at Ephesus, in the midst of one of his most successful church planting initiatives, Paul was writing to believers in Rome whom he had never met. He had always wanted to visit with them, but he told them he never wanted to build on another man's foundation, that he was always committed to going where there had been no previous gospel witness (Rom. 15:20, 21). He then says, "For this reason I have often been prevented from coming to you, but now, with no further place for me in these regions (in Asia Minor, modern day western Turkey), and since I have had for many years a longing to come to you whenever I go to Spain, for I hope to see you in passing, and to be helped on my way there by you" (Rom. 15:22-24). He says earlier in Romans 15:19 that he has fully preached the gospel from Jerusalem all the way to Illyricum (modern day Croatia). Paul saw no conflict whatsoever between the sovereignty of God and our responsibility to take the gospel to the whole world. Consider the astonishing amount of work Paul accomplished as it is portrayed in this timeline of his ministry:

- Conversion on the road to Damascus, AD 31
- Ministry in Damascus and Arabia (Nabataea), 31 to AD 33
- Ministry in Cilicia and Syria, AD 34 to 42
- Ministry in Antioch, AD 42 to 44
- First Missionary Journey to southern region of Galatia, AD 45 to 47
- Jerusalem Council, AD 48
- Second Missionary Journey to Europe, AD 49 to 51
- Third Missionary Journey to Asia Minor, AD 52 to 57
- Arrested in Jerusalem, AD 57
- Imprisonment in Caesarea, AD 57 to 59
- Imprisonment in Rome, AD 60 to 62
- Brief release (see 2 Tim. 4:16) from prison where he may have made it to Spain, AD 63
- Ministry with Titus on island of Crete (Titus 1:5), AD 64 to 65 and Nicopolis in Italy (Titus 3:12)
- Arrested a second time and martyred in Rome by Emperor Nero, AD 66 to 67

Then think for a moment of the sheer number of miles Paul traveled, mainly on foot, but sometimes by ship. As an example, if we trace his second missionary journey from Jerusalem to

Antioch to Pisidian Antioch to Troas to Philippi to Athens to Corinth to Ephesus to Caesarea to Jerusalem and to Antioch (about three years, Acts 15:30 to 18:22), then we find that he traveled 1933 miles on foot and 1280 miles by ship.

What drove this man? What can we learn from him? He received his divine commission from the resurrected Jesus. He was a chosen instrument of Christ's to bear His name before Gentiles, kings, and the sons of Israel. Jesus showed him how much he must suffer for His sake (Acts 9:15). Jesus told Paul in a dream that he was no longer to be afraid in Corinth. Instead, he was to keep on preaching the gospel. No one would harm him there. There would be many conversions (Acts 18:11). He received his ministry from the Lord Jesus to testify solemnly to the gospel of the grace of God (Acts 20:24). Paul knew that he was under obligation to preach the gospel. He was eager to do so because he was not ashamed of the gospel. Why not? Because he knew it alone was the power of God for salvation (Rom. 1:14-16). There was no other way. In fact, he clearly stated that he was accursed if he refused to preach the gospel, "Woe is me if I do not preach the gospel" (1 Cor. 9:16). The love of Christ, Christ's love for Paul, and Paul's love for Christ, drove him incessantly, compelled him to take every opportunity to preach Christ to as many people as he possibly could (2 Cor. 5:14,15).

So, what must your church do? What must you do as church leaders to keep the main thing the main thing? You have no alternative. You must get outside the four walls of the church building. You must go to the eighty percent of the people in this country who do not attend church, meeting lost people, listening to them, engaging them in gospel conversation, weeping with them as they tell you their stories, seeing the devastation of what a life of sinful rebellion against God and His word has wrought. This will give you the edge to go far, fast, and furious with the gospel.

Charles Spurgeon, the great 19th century Baptist preacher, said, "Heresies in the Christian church come never from the city missionary, never from the faithful pastor, never from the intense evangelist; but always from gentlemen at ease who take no actual part in our holy war." The problem with progressivism in the church comes from the intellectual elites who in their pride think they know best, that the plain-spoken preacher or evangelist is simple-minded and really does not understand the modern man. We must, however, be thrust out into the world and be willing to suffer hardship, rejection, ridicule, and perhaps even physical harm for the sake of Christ and His gospel, all the while being motivated by the glorious fact that Jesus gave Himself up for our transgressions and was raised for our justification. There is no other way, my friends. Get out of your comfort zone. Go far, fast, and furious with the gospel of grace. This clearly is what the Scriptures teach.

There is one more very practical principle to glean from the apostles in their calling to make disciples of all the nations, and this principle fits very well with the office of evangelist. You will note in Acts 13, after Paul was fetched by Barnabas from Tarsus, that he joined Barnabas in serving the church at Antioch. However, after a year or two of ministry there, the elders laid hands on Paul and Barnabas and sent them out as missionaries, what we might call an Apostolic band or a missionary band. The elders at Antioch laid hands on Paul and Barnabas, ordaining them for their ministry. They also prayed and fasted for them and sent them on their way (Acts 13:1-3). We then read in Acts 13:4ff of their ministry on the island of Cyprus and then into Turkey and the Galatian region.

What does this mean practically to you who are leaders in the local church? Paul and Barnabas were uniquely gifted men. Paul in particular was called by Jesus as an apostle and he clearly was a gifted evangelist. He went far, fast, and furious with the gospel, as we have noted earlier in this chapter. Not everyone in the church was gifted or called to do what Paul did. Most of the believers in Paul's day were local church people, committed to the ministry of the gospel in their respective communities. And this, of course, is normal and good. There are men, however, whom God has uniquely gifted and called for a type of apostolic ministry. By this I do not mean they are modern day apostles as were Paul and the disciples of Jesus. That's because the gifts of apostle and prophet in the gospels and Acts were revelatory gifts (see Eph. 2:20-22) which are no longer needed and therefore no longer in existence because we have a fully canonical Bible. Nonetheless, there are men whom God raises up at certain times in the church who are gifted to lead a movement. We see this in the life of John Calvin, George Whitefield, John Wesley, Charles Spurgeon, Billy Graham, Martin Lloyd-Jones, and R.C. Sproul. There are also other men from other nations, men whom you do not know, whom God is raising up to be church planting leaders in places like India, Africa, and China. These are men we might call apostles with a small letter *a*.

So, what does this have to do with you, church leader? Pray for God to supply you with evangelists, men whom God has uniquely gifted as evangelists and perhaps apostles with a small letter *a*. Then send them out with your blessing, prayers, and financial support. Give them the freedom to reach out to whomever God directs them. Do not micromanage them. Do not put them in an administrative or pastoral role. They are not administrators. They are not pastors. If possible, supply them with a full-time or at least a part-time salary or stipend to help them with their living expenses. After all, Paul says a workman is worthy of his wages (1 Tim. 5:18). As these evangelists go to the streets of your city or community, whether it be in door-to-door evangelistic work, open air preaching, or some other avenue of service, give them the freedom to do what God has called them to do. These men will take a few people with them, training them to do the same thing they were taught to do.

There needs to be a major paradigm shift in the American church. At best, our discipleship training is merely addition. We disciple a person or two who grow in the grace and knowledge of the Lord. That, of course, is good but it is not enough. We must intentionally move toward the multiplication of disciples. We must find men and women to disciple who, in turn, will disciple others who will disciple others who will disciple others. Paul clearly gives us that admonition and example when he says to his disciple Timothy, "The things you have learned from me in the presence of many witnesses, these entrust to faithful men who will be able to teach others also" (2 Tim. 2:2).

Before moving on to the next chapter, we need to ask you an important question—do you have a missionary band of people in your church who regularly go to the streets of your city to preach evangelistic messages and to evangelize one-on-one or door-to-door? If not, then why not ask God to bring you people like that and then to pray for them, lay hands on them, and support them financially to evangelize in your community and city? Do you have this band of evangelists? Then why not do everything in your capacity to unleash them into your community?

Advice for Churches— Training and Sending

We tend to read Acts with our own cultural and theological "glasses." Unwittingly, we read Acts with a bias. May we strongly suggest, at this point, that you and your church officers commit to reading the book of Acts as though you have never read it before? We are asking you to read it with a blank slate, so to speak. Try your best to put yourself into the time when Luke wrote it. Take the book one chapter at a time. Read it slowly and carefully and record what you see. This will prepare for us for the topic of training and sending evangelists.

The importance of the Holy Spirit

For example, consider what is happening in Acts 2 on the day of Pentecost. After Jesus' ascension into heaven, the one hundred and twenty gathered together in the Upper Room and prayed for ten days until the promised Holy Spirit came upon them. They began to speak in other tongues as the Spirit was giving them utterance (Acts 2:4). In other words, all one hundred and twenty were speaking in other known languages so that all the Jews from far off places who were gathered together in Jerusalem for the Feast of First Fruits of the wheat harvest could hear the praise of God in their own language. From there we know that Peter preached the gospel to them, and they were pierced in the heart. They were deeply convicted of their own sin and the judgment under which they were living, and they were fearful to stand before the Holy One. They asked what they must do, and Peter said, "Repent, and each of you be baptized in the name of Jesus Christ for the forgiveness of your sins; and you will receive the gift of the Holy Spirit" (Acts 2:38). We are then told that those who had received Peter's word were baptized immediately and about three thousand souls were added that day to the church.

What do you notice here that we usually do not find in our churches today? Several things jump out. First, they were engaged in extraordinary prayer, diligently seeking God for ten days for the Holy Spirit's presence and power. We seldom pray like that in the western church. Then you will notice a powerful manifestation of the Holy Spirit coming upon all the people. We should also expect people to be pierced in the heart by our preaching, street evangelism, or our door-to-door work. We should believe that God through the Holy Spirit is going before us in our labors and preparing people to hear the gospel preached to them and to respond in repentance and faith. My friends, do you expect this to happen when you speak to others about their souls? You should certainly pray for that and expect it.

One other thing. You will notice that the people who called on the name of the Lord on that day were baptized immediately. You will notice the same thing with the Ethiopian eunuch in Acts 8, when Phillip preaches Jesus to him (Acts 8:25-38). And the Philippian jailer and his household were all baptized when he believed on Christ (Acts 16:33). Baptism is so much a part of the cultural experience in the United States that I fear it has lost its significance. It typically doesn't cost anything. When one is baptized in a Muslim or Hindu culture, it is a very big deal. Very often it means death or at the very least estrangement from the family. Why? Because baptism means a departure from one's former way of living and a wholehearted commitment to making Jesus our King, Lord, Savior, and Redeemer. Baptism is identification with Christ. It is a vivid picture of the washing away of our sins and the gift of the Holy Spirit coming upon the new believer.

There are many more lessons for us to learn from Acts, but here's the point—if we are to train our people to be sincere followers of Jesus Christ then we must go back to the original source, the Bible, and lay aside our traditions. Also, what we read there we must purpose to believe and obey.

Multiplying evangelists

Secondly in this matter of training, we must be committed to the multiplication of disciples. How do we do this? Consider the acrostic MAWL, which stands for model, assist, watch, and leave. This is the key to multiplication. We see this in the ministry of our Lord Jesus with His disciples. Luke begins Acts by writing, "The first account I composed, Theophilus, about all Jesus began to do and teach" (Acts 1:1). Notice Luke does not say "all that Jesus began to teach and do." Jesus modeled to His disciples His ministry of preaching, teaching, evangelizing, and showing mercy.

We are to do the same, but how? As an example, when I go out to engage in open air preaching, I make every effort possible to bring along a young man or two who has never preached before in the open air. I want him to come and see what we do. Likewise, when I go door-to-door in a neighborhood, I again try to bring one or two young men with me. I say to them, "You don't have to say anything. Just watch what I do." For some of us, including me, this is counterintuitive. Most pastors or evangelists are pretty accomplished at what they do, and they really do not want to take the time to bring other men along in learning how to preach or evangelize. It is like the great baseball player Hank Aaron. He never tried to be a manager or coach. Hitting came natural to him and he probably did not have the patience to teach others what he was so accomplished at doing. Church leaders need to be proactive in this matter of multiplication. Growth by addition is so ingrained in the psyche and practice of most church leaders that this will be a very difficult thing to do. Yet, it is vital if we are serious in reaching this nation with the glorious gospel of our Lord Jesus Christ.

So, after we have been modeling evangelizing and preaching, we then should make a concerted effort to assist the disciple in learning how to do the same. This takes time. We should take a few young men with us when we preach or go door-to-door. After we have modeled this a few times and explained what we are doing and why, then we can say, "May I teach you how to do the same?" We then spend a few weeks going over how practically to preach or evangelize one-on-one. We practice with our disciples.

Then, we watch what they do. Let them know that you are not going to throw them into the deep end of the pool and let them sink. You will be right there beside them to rescue them if they become fearful or do not know what to say or how to respond to a skeptic. After that, we get with them and go over what they did right and what they could improve on. We always want to be positive and affirming to our disciples. Begin by telling them what they did well, then speak of the things they can do better and suggest how they might actually do the exercise better. Then finish with another word of encouragement. Watch them several times, and then you are ready to leave them. By this, we do not mean that you desert them, but we do mean that you send them out to do what you have taught them to do. They are to repeat the MAWL process with a few disciples of their own.

I remember several years ago watching two sparrows prepare a nest under the eve of our house. Soon, eggs were in the nest and the mother and father took turns sitting on the eggs. And then I remember watching the three baby birds hatching from their eggs. Soon, they were standing on the side of the nest, gathering the courage to jump off and fly. The first two went quickly with no trouble. The third baby bird, however, was pretty reluctant. He stood on the side of the nest for several minutes. Finally, the mother bird gently nudged him off the next and away he flew without difficulty. This is the way we should approach the training of our disciples. After we have modeled the skill, after we have given them serious attention in teaching them what to do, after we have watched them and evaluated with them their progress, then we let them go on their own.

We need to spend a little more time here focusing on the sending. As they leave the nest, so to speak, what are they to do in the context of evangelistic ministry? I am focusing here mainly on two aspects of evangelistic ministry. The first is open air preaching and the second is door-to-door evangelism. Both are vital to any church. As we noted earlier, open air preaching is akin to carpet bombing in World War II. It is a broadcast of the gospel. On the other hand, door-to-door evangelism is like having troops on the ground, going from street-to-street, door-to-door, confronting and subduing the enemy.

Open air Preaching

Let's look first at open air preaching. Perhaps you have a friend whose husband is in serious trouble with COVID-19. He is on a ventilator and your friend is not allowed in the hospital to see her very ill husband. You have spoken the good news of Jesus Christ to her, telling her that she, her husband, and their children are indeed sinners who have broken God's law and they are facing the certain, terrifying expectation of judgment in hell. She has politely listened, but has never called upon the name of the Lord Jesus to save her. Now she is beside herself with fear and worry. She has no hope, and she is without God in this world.

I was open air preaching a while back at Toomer's Corner in Auburn, and also at the stadium before an Auburn football game. The students were very respectful. Auburn kids are some of the nicest I have ever encountered on a college campus. Most of these young people would claim to be Christians, and I am sure some of them are. However, we encountered at least one young man who claimed to be a Christian, but admitted living with his girlfriend. We told him that fornicators will not inherit the kingdom of God, that he must repent, or he is in danger of hellfire. Though the young man is receiving a quality education, though he certainly has hopes of a good, well-paying job upon graduation, and though he no doubt hopes to marry one day, rear children, and live a long life, he still has no real hope, and he is without God in this world.

The homosexual, the drunkard, the thief, the con artist, the moralist, the Mormon, the Hindu, the Muslim, the racist, the nice atheist and the Marxist all share this in common—they are dead in trespasses and sins, having no hope and without God in this world. Of course, no one can live long without some kind of hope. Those who commit suicide have given up hope. But the hope of unbelievers is no hope at all. It is bogus. It is counterfeit. It is a mirage. The hope of such people will not prevail when they stand before the Holy One and give account of every deed they have done in the body, whether good or bad. The whole unbelieving world lies in the power of the evil one. They are blinded by the devil. They are living according to the course of this world, according to the prince of the power of the air, according to the spirit of the one who is now working in the sons of disobedience (all unconverted people). Such people are constantly indulging the desires of their own flesh and mind. They are children of wrath just like everyone else. Because they are dead in their sins, they have no hunger for truth, they have no thirst for righteousness. Because they have suppressed the truth of God in unrighteousness God has consequently given them over in the lusts of their hearts to impurity. God has given them over to the degrading passions of homosexual perversion. And furthermore, God has given them over to reprobate and depraved minds so that they are filled with wickedness, evil, greed, murder, strife, deceit, malice. They are haters of God, insolent, arrogant, boastful, inventors of evil.

We see this horrible description of the unconverted man played out every day in our cities, towns, universities, seats of government, and the business world. While any Presidential election is vitally important and very often determines whether or not we move closer to socialism or whether or not the scourge of abortion may be overturned, we still know good government at best can only slow down the putrefaction in our nation. Government and politics can never cleanse a nation. They are only capable of administering justice and protecting her people from domestic violence and crime and from invasion of foreign enemies.

My friends, the very fact that God has not wiped the United States off the face of the earth in one swift move of judgment is a testimony to His long-suffering patience. We have sinned horribly. We are wicked and perverse. Sex-trafficking, abortion, corruption, lawlessness, and all manner of perversion, in the face of God's great goodness and abundance, ought to move us to repentance. Instead, we continue to spit in the face of Him who has supplied us richly with all things to enjoy.

Where are we going with all of this? These are many of the reasons we need street preachers all over the United States, preaching daily wherever they can, proclaiming the unfathomable riches of Christ. People tell us that street preaching does not work in today's secular world, that people don't like it, that we are infringing on people's rights of privacy, that such preaching is out of place, uncivil, that it refuses to engage in civil discourse, that surely there is a better way to reach people than to "bludgeon" them with the gospel.

To be sure, there are some bad actors preaching on the streets, those who preach hate, legalism, or antinomianism.

They should surely be resisted or ignored, but men who preach the doctrine of God, the total depravity of man, the glory, power, and efficacy of Christ's person and work, who passionately, unequivocally, and freely offer the gospel to everyone, calling them to repent and believe on Christ, must be encouraged, strengthened, and supported.

The simple fact is that God has always used preaching as His means of converting the elect. Open air preaching has never been popular. The people of Jeremiah's day hated it. The people of Jesus' day despised it and crucified the Savior. Paul was beaten many times for engaging in it. George Whitefield was mocked for doing it. Openair preaching, if done under the leading of the Holy Spirit, does work. The word of God never returns empty. It always accomplishes its purpose. It brings salvation to some, but those who reject it face a greater judgment. We are not infringing on people's privacy when we preach in the open air. It is never intrusion to warn a man who is looking at his cell phone as he crosses a street in front of an oncoming truck. We are not preaching hate. We are preaching the greatest, most wonderful news in the world, and when people hate preaching, then we know they hate the God whom we are proclaiming.

Open air preaching is not the only form of evangelism, but it is the first and necessary way to get the gospel to the world. It brings light to those in darkness. It pricks the conscience of those who hear it. It softens up the elect for the day when the Spirit opens their eyes to see, giving them ears to hear, granting them the grace to repent and believe. There is a time for dialogue with unbelievers. Any street preacher will tell you that people do stop and listen, that they sometimes do have sincere questions, and that is the time to go one-on-one with them.

Street preaching is to lead the way. Churches and pastors who do not support street preachers are typically lax in their ministries. Without this intentional evangelistic work, the seeds of death are already being sown in the life of the church. It may have a multi-million-dollar budget with a beautiful building, and outstanding programs, but death is already present. It may take ten or twenty years, but the church will surely die. Street preaching must lead the way.

One-to-one evangelism

But we must also go further and say that we must train and send our people out to engage in one-on-one evangelism, whether it is survey evangelism in a town center, door-to-door in neighborhoods, or intentional tract distribution in a park. We know what many church pundits are saying—intentional, 'drive by' evangelism does not work anymore. People are too secular for this kind of thing. What we need to do is to develop relationships with people by joining a local workout facility, spend time with the people, and then eventually earn the right to tell them about Jesus. Of course we are to build relationships with people, and of course we should be good and kind neighbors who bring in our neighbor's trash cans and mail when they are on vacation. However, being kind neighbors and intentional in our evangelism are not mutually exclusive. Why can't we do both?

Besides, ask yourself this question—is that what you see in the ministry of the Lord Jesus and His apostles? Did Jesus or the apostles sit in *Starbucks* waiting for people to ask them questions about their faith? Even a cursory reading of the gospels and Acts makes clear that they were always moving, always engaging people in the gospel. Paul went to the local market and spoke daily to the people there in Athens. He told the Ephesian elders that he did not shrink from declaring to them anything profitable, that he was teaching them publicly and from house-to-house.

Every church and every pastor ought to have a plan to visit regularly and systematically every household within a two to three mile radius of the church building. Here's what we are after—a church setting aside two hours per week to go door-to-door and seek to engage people with the gospel. We have already stressed the need for missionary bands sponsored by the church to go out regularly to the community. Now, however, we are also suggesting that the pastor give this kind of work an hour or two per week. But you may object, "I am a busy pastor or elder. I don't have the time." Make the time. You want to have an apostolic ministry, don't you? Then do what the apostles did. You may further object, "People in my community are hard-hearted, affluent, and secular. I will never get a hearing from them by knocking on their door. They will simply dismiss me as a Jehovah's Witness or Mormon." Our answer? Who cares what people think? This is the model Jesus gives when he sends out the seventy in Luke 10, telling them to look for people of peace, people who are willing to receive them into their homes. When I work with churches that ask me to help them with their evangelism, I always stress door-to-door evangelism. I say, "When we go out today, we are looking for the one out of ten, or one out of one hundred who are open to hear about Jesus. We know that the Holy Spirit must open people up to the gospel, that left to their own devices they are not buying what we are selling. But we have prayed, asking God to lead us to people who are open. And without fail, I always find at least one good contact from each session of door-to-door witnessing."

In his book *Fanatical Prospecting,* Jeb Blount is speaking to salesmen of all kinds, and telling them that they must make cold calls every day. He says that nobody wants to do this, that he himself hates doing it, but it is still the most effective way to get prospects into one's pipeline. Every salesman has quarterly or yearly sales numbers he is expected to reach. To be success-ful, he must work daily to get potential sales prospects. Why? Because it usually takes a long time to complete a sale. If the salesman has no one in his pipeline, then he will not sell any-thing, and his family will starve. If he waits to the last week of the quarter or year to make contacts, then he is in big trouble. There is not enough time or prospects to make the necessary sales. Why is evangelism any different? This is not to say we should get our ideas from secular salesmen, but rather, why is it that secular salesmen are willing to risk looking dumb or obnoxious for the sake of money, whereas many Christians are not willing to do so for the sake of an eternal soul?

Here's our challenge—pastor, elder, or deacon, give two hours per week to go into the surrounding community of your church and knock on doors. Take one or two other people with you. At least one needs to be a woman if you go in threes. Three men at one's door makes many people pretty nervous. Map the streets, keep meticulous records, and go. What do you say?

There are two approaches which I like. First, introduce yourself and those with you, telling your neighbor your church's name and location. You can say, "We are seeking to get to know more people in our community and we would like to do a better of job of serving our community. May I ask you a question? Is there anything we can pray for you about? Or to put it another way, if God would do a miracle for you right now, what would it be?" If the person gives me a request, I write it down with their name and cell number and pray a brief prayer for them on the spot. I then briefly give my testimony, in less than one minute and ask, "Do you have a story like that?" If they say "no," then you have a pretty good idea that the person is not yet a Christian. Then you can invite them to church or let them know you're willing to have a Bible study with them and others in the neighborhood. Ask them if they think that is something they would be interested in. If they say, "yes," then give the person the information about the church or Bible study and get back with him later. If you get a "no," then don't worry about it and move on to the next house. If people are rude or will not engage with you, don't worry about it. Don't be discouraged. Remember, you are looking for the one out ten, the one out of a hundred. You are looking for the person of peace.

Think about it—if a church spent only two hours per week and found one person of peace each week, then by the end of the year the church may have forty or fifty "gospel prospects" in their pipeline. And then the various gifts of the church could work together. For example, if your visits find a person whose house is in disrepair, but you discern that they do not have the money to repair it, then you could find a ministry in your city which serves people in such a situation. You could continue to reach out to that person or family. We are certain such a ministry of mercy would open that family to the gospel of grace. Or you may find an older woman who just lost her husband to Alzheimer's and she is lonely. You have people in your church who have the gift of mercy and who could visit with this woman and befriend her.

Conclusion

The reason why "evangelist" is such a dirty word in Reformed circles likely has something to do with itinerants who have no connection with any local church and typically use more rhetoric and emotion than biblical persuasion. Easy-believism, revivalism, gimmicks, pragmatism, and Arminianism in large part could be a result of popular "evangelists" endorsing such methods. But this is no reason to dismiss the office as a result. It would be unfair to say that because Joel Osteen, Kenneth Copeland, and Benny Hinn are typically referred to as pastors, the office itself has been irrecoverably tainted and hence should no longer cease to exist. But that is what we have done when it comes to the evangelist.

Another reason could be certain parachurch ministries, which evangelists are commonly associated with. Most full-time evangelists operate using a parachurch approach, since most churches are unable or unwilling to support them. But again, when we consider that the evangelist has been relegated to a fringe position in the church, should we expect anything different? Many churches are willing to staff several full-time pastors at a time, which is great, but very few could boast of having even a single evangelist. In fact, among Reformed churches, it would be poor taste to officially recognize someone as an evangelist, since doing so would be to reject Calvin and the Puritans on the subject. The evangelist is then scuttled away, out of the realm of relevance. This leads to an obsessively inward-looking milieu among Reformed churches.

The West needs to be evangelized more than ever before, but we are fighting the battle without a necessary officer. Most churches have at least one elder-qualified man who has a burden for evangelism, both doing it and teaching others how to do it. Rather than keeping them quiet or merely outside with the lost, it is time to recognize their gift, ordain them, and let them do what the ascended Christ has equipped them to do—teach the saints about evangelism, lead the saints in the work of evangelism, and protect the saints from unbiblical evangelism. The pastor can do this too, true, but rarely is the pastor able to distill the importance of evangelism into an entire church culture. By his very gifting, the pastor is more inward looking. He appreciates evangelism. He may do the work of an evangelist. But he is not an evangelist. He is a pastor.

The Reformed church has been unbalanced in its approach to evangelism, but it is not too late to do something about it. Is there any wonder why the very lands where the Reformation had most sway are now haunted by atheism, the occult, homosexuality, abortion, and every other kind of evil under the sun? Is it any wonder that the church has lost its edge when it comes to evangelizing the lost when the office of evangelist has been deemed "extraordinary," rather than permanent? Is it any wonder that our churches in the Reformed community are by and large much smaller and less potent than those who utilize the office of evangelist? It is time to correct our wrong by reanalyzing what Scripture says about this officer and what church history has shown whenever this officer is relegated to the sidelines.

Evangelism is usually not spoken about at conferences. It is rarely emphasized by even the most biblical pastors and teachers. By reinstating the office of evangelist to the place which Christ has intended, these problems can be addressed. By giving evangelists a place among pastors and teachers, evangelism will be more in the forefront of our churches. The church will become better "gospellers." The lost will be confronted with more urgency. More people will hear the name of Christ. God's glory will resound all the more exuberantly. True, evangelists are different. They are less tame. They can cause headaches and shake up the status-quo. But they can also be harnessed and unleashed upon our communities, heralding Christ to those who have ears and to those who don't, which is exactly what Christ intended when He gave some to be evangelists.

About the Authors

AL BAKER is ordained in Vanguard Presbytery and has been in the gospel ministry for over thirty-five years. Al's ministry base of operation is Birmingham, Alabama, serving as an Evangelist with Reformed Evangelistic Fellowship (formerly PEF). Al is the author of several books. Al has long been actively involved in foreign missions, also traveling extensively around the United States preaching in churches and in the streets. Al and Wini have been married since 1975 and have three grown sons, three daughter-in-laws, and twelve grandchildren.

RYAN DENTON was a pastor on the Navajo Reservation before starting *Christ in the Wild Ministries*. He is a church planter and evangelist in Texas. He is the author of several books.